BIBLE AND TALMUD STORIES

A BIBLICAL HISTORY FOR SCHOOL AND HOME

WITH

STORIES FROM THE TALMUD AND MIDRASH,
QUESTIONS, MAPS AND ILLUSTRATIONS

BY

HYMAN E. GOLDIN

VOLUME I
FROM THE BEGINNING TO THE DEATH OF MOSES

STAR HEBREW BOOK COMPANY
54-58 CANAL STREET
NEW YORK CITY

Printed in the United States of America

Printed in the United States of America

PREFACE

"BIBLE AND TALMUD STORIES" is designed to acquaint the student with the narrative portion of the Bible, the contents of which has proved to be a source of inexhaustible delight to the world, Jew and non-Jew alike, for a great many centuries.

With this object in view, the author has made an endeavor: a) to give the story in full, not omitting any of the incidents recorded in the Holy Book; b) to divide the narration into convenient chapters, which are followed by questions; c) to present the stories in a simple, interesting style; d) and, above all, to maintain the matchless beauty of the original whenever possible.

To further stimulate the interest of the student in the study of the history of the Holy Book, the author has supplemented many chapters with stories from the Talmud and Midrash. From the great store of legends woven about the heroes and stories of the Bible, the author has selected only some of those which have an intense human feeling and deep religious thoughts.

H. E. G.

New York, May, 1931.

CONTENTS

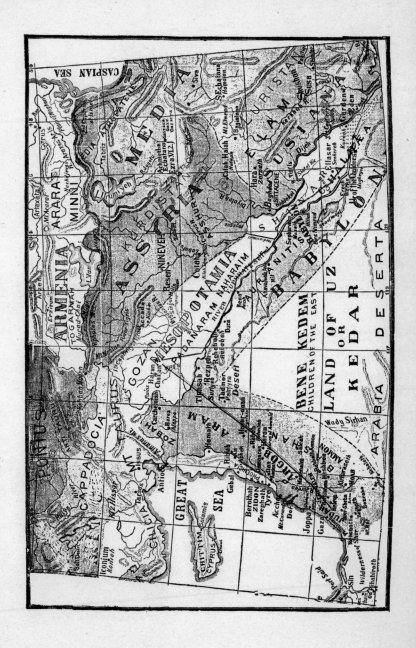

I
IN THE BEGINNING

Long, long ago there was nothing in existence, no earth, no heavens and no stars. There was only the Supreme Being, God, and he, by the word of his mouth, brought everything into existence.

God created the world in six days. First he created the heaven and the earth, but the earth was covered by water and lay in darkness. God then said: "Let there be light," and light at once appeared. When God saw that the light was good, he called the light Day, and the darkness he called Night. All this took place on the first day of the creation.

On the second day, God created the firmament, which he called Heaven. But water still covered the surface of the earth, and there was no dry land visible.

On the third day, God said: "Let the water covering the earth be gathered into one place, so that dry land may be seen." Immediately the water formed seas, lakes and rivers, and dry land became visible. By the command of God, grass, trees and other vegetation appeared on the earth.

On the fourth day, the stars and the planets were set in the sky, by the word of God. He ordered the sun to shine during the day, and the moon and the stars to shine at night.

There were as yet no animals in existence. On the fifth day of the creation, God created the fish in the water and the winged fowl in the air. God then blessed the first animate beings with the words: "Be fruitful and multiply."

On the sixth day, God created all kinds of animals. Finally God said: "I will create a man who shall possess wisdom and be superior to all creatures." God then created the man with his own hands. He formed the first man out of the dust of the ground, and breathed into him a living soul. He gave the man power and wisdom, so that he might be the master of all the creatures on earth. The first human being was named Adam, because he was created from earth (in Hebrew, *adamah*.)

Thus, God created the heavens and the earth and everything they contain in six days, and on the seventh day he rested. For this reason God blessed the seventh day and made it holy. He commanded us to rest on the seventh day of the week, and he called this day Sabbath (in Hebrew it means rest).

AGADAH*)

God Dislikes Jealousy

When first created, the light of the moon was equal to that of the sun. The moon became envious of the sun. She presented herself before God and complained: "Master of the World, you have created two luminaries, and you have given to both the same amount of light. How will one be able to distinguish one from the other? Is it not becoming that one luminary should be greater than the other, so that one should be able to tell which is the sun and which is the moon?"

"I know", said God, "that you would have me make you greater than the sun. Therefore your light shall henceforth be reduced, and all living beings shall know that the smaller light is the moon, and the greater light is the sun."

"Must I be punished so severely for having spoken a few words?" protested the moon.

"In time to come," said God, "I shall make your light again equal to that of the sun."

"O Lord," said the envious moon, "and the light of the sun, how great will it be then?"

"What! You still plot against the sun?" asked

---

* Legendary part of the Talmud.

God. "Verily, in time to come, his light shall be sevenfold the light he now sheds."

The moon thereupon wailed before God and complained: "The punishment meted out to me is greater than I can bear."

God in reply said: "You shall not be alone in the sky. I shall set the stars in the skies to accompany you on your journey at night."

QUESTIONS

1) Who existed before the world was created?
2) In how many days did God create the world?
3) When did God create the light, and how?
4) What was created on the second day?
5) When were the seas, lakes and rivers formed?
6) What did God do on the fourth day?
7) What kind of animate beings did God create on the fifth day?
8) What were created on the sixth day?
9) Why was the first man called Adam?
10) Why did God make the seventh day holy?
11) Why is the seventh day called Sabbath?

II
THE FIRST CRIME

Adam was alone in this great, wide world, and God said: "It is not good for the man to be alone." So, one day, when Adam was fast asleep, God took a rib from his side, and from the rib he created a woman. When the woman was brought by God to Adam, he called her name Eve (Havah, Life).

Far, away, somewheres in the East, God planted a beautiful garden. The garden was full of trees bearing lovely fruit, and of very beautiful flowers which diffused the air with their fragrance. Through the middle of the garden, there flowed a river, full of fresh crystal-clear water. This beautiful spot was called "The Garden of Eden."

God placed Adam and Eve into that beautiful garden, and said to them: "Look at the very charming home I have made for you to live in. You may stay here all the time, and you may eat of all the fruit that grows in the garden. But one thing I want you to bear in mind. Yonder in the middle of the garden stand two trees, the tree of life and the tree of knowledge. Of the fruit of the tree of knowledge you may not eat. Should you disobey me and eat of its fruit, you shall die."

Adam and Eve in the Garden of Eden

The first human couple lived happily in the garden of Eden. They were just like a pair of happy children, who knew neither shame, nor sorrow, nor fear, nor evil. But their happiness was short-lived, and troubles soon set in for Adam and his wife.

One day, the serpent, who was the most cunning of all animals, said to Eve: "Why do you not eat some of the delicious fruit that grows on the tree yonder in the middle of the garden?"

"God commanded us not to eat it," replied Eve. "He even told us not to touch it. He said that if we eat this fruit, we shall surely die."

"This is not true," said the serpent. "You will not die when you eat this fruit. If you and your husband taste this fruit, you will be very wise. Like God himself you will have the understanding of good and evil. That is why God told you not to eat it. He is simply envious; he does not want you to become as wise as he is."

Eve could resist the temptation no longer. She picked some of the fruit of the tree of knowledge, and ate it. She even gave some of the fruit to Adam, and he too ate it. Now, that they disobeyed the command of God and sinned, they began to feel shame and fear. Their eyes were opened, and they began to understand things that they had not understood before. They realized for the first time that they were naked, and they made for themselves coverings of fig-leaves.

Suddenly Adam and Eve heard some one come in the garden. They knew that they had sinned, and they were afraid. So they hid themselves among the trees of the garden.

"Adam, where are you?" asked a stern, powerful voice. For, it was God who thus spoke.

"We were ashamed, because we were naked," answered Adam, "and therefore we hid ourselves among the trees."

"And who told you that you were naked?" inquired God. "Have you eaten of the fruit of the tree which I bade you not to eat?"

Adam answered: "The woman whom you gave to be with me, she gave me from the fruit of the tree, and I ate it."

"What have you done?" God said to the woman.

Eve answered: "The serpent persuaded me and I ate."

God punished the wily serpent. God told him that he could never walk on his feet as the other animals do, but would have to crawl on the ground; and that his food shall be the dust of the ground all his life.

To the woman God said: "I will greatly increase your sorrows; in pain shall you bring forth children."

Adam, too, received his punishment. God said to him: "Because you have hearkened to the voice of your wife, the ground shall be cursed for your sake. In the sweat of your brow shall you eat bread, till you return to the ground; for dust you are, and to dust shall you return."

God thereupon made coats of skin for Adam and his wife, and clothed them.

After that God ordered Adam and Eve out of the garden of Eden, and at the entrance of the garden he placed an angel with a fiery sword to guard the way to the tree of life, "lest he put forth his hand, and take also of the tree of life, and eat, and live forever." From that time on, Adam and Eve were forced to live by the toil of their hands, tilling the ground for their bread.

AGADAH

Laugh Not at the Misfortune of Others

When Adam and Eve ate of the tree of knowledge and became aware of their nakedness, they wept bitterly. With them wept the clouds, the sun, the planets, the stars and all created things. Even the angels in heaven grieved over the fall of man. The moon alone laughed.

When God punished the serpent, Adam and Eve for their disobedience, the moon, too, received her punishment. God said to her: "Because you alone laughed at the fall of man, while all other creatures had pity on him, your light shall be obscured. Instead of shining steadily like the sun, you shall grow old quickly, and you shall be born and die every month."

QUESTIONS

1) What was the name of the first woman, and why was she so named?
2) Where did God place the first couple, and what did he command them?
3) What did the serpent say to Eve?
4) Was it true that God had commanded Eve not to touch the tree of knowledge?
5) What did Adam and Eve feel after they had sinned?
6) What was the serpent's punishment?
7) What was Eve's punishment?
8) What was Adam's punishment?

III
THE FIRST MURDER

Adam and Eve had two sons; the firstborn was named Cain, and the second one was named Abel. Cain was always sad and gloomy; Abel, on the other hand, was always happy and gay. When the two brothers grew up, Cain became a farmer, a tiller of the soil, and Abel became a shepherd, tending sheep and cattle.

One day, Cain and Abel thought of the good God in heaven, and desired to thank him for his kindness. They wanted to thank him for the good things he had given them, and at the same time pray to him. They could think of no other way of thanking God than by offering him some of the things they themselves loved best. So Cain, being a farmer, offered some of the fruit of the ground as a sacrifice to God. Abel, being a shepherd, offered from the best of his flock as a sacrifice to God.

God hates sad, gloomy and dissatisfied people, and therefore he did not accept Cain's offering.

But he accepted the sacrifice of Abel who was always pleased, happy and contented.

Abel Lay Lifelessly at Cain's Feet

Cain somehow felt that God had accepted Abel's sacrifice, but had refused his. Cain now realized that his brother was a better man than he. But instead of loving his brother and learning from him to be good, Cain became envious of his brother. He grew very uneasy, and often evil thoughts would flash through his mind.

One day, Cain heard God's voice whisper to him: "Cain, why are you angry, and why are you unhappy? You only try to do well, and your drooping spirit will be raised. But if you make no attempt to do well, sin will get hold of you at all times. Still, even then you will always be able to overcome sin, if you only try."

But Cain did not heed the wonderful advice God had given him. Instead, he kept on nursing his grudge against his noble brother, until one day, when they were alone in the field, Cain struck his brother with all his might. Abel immediately fell to the ground, and lay lifelessly at Cain's feet.

Cain was amazed to see his brother remain motionless, for he hardly realized what he had done. Cain was finally awakened from his stupor by a powerful voice, the voice of God: "Cain, where is your brother Abel?" In anger and fright, Cain answered: "I do not know where he is. Am I my brother's keeper?" The voice of God said once more: "Cain, what have you done? The voice of your brother's blood cries to me from the ground. You shall be punished for your crime and become a wanderer on the earth."

"Alas, my punishment is so great that I am unable to bear it!" cried the unhappy Cain. "If I have to remain a wanderer all my life, I will be killed by any one who meets me!"

God thereupon set a mark on Cain's face as a warning that no one should dare slay him. And Cain became a wanderer for ever. He could find rest at no place. Wherever he came, he heard an accusing gentle voice asking in his heart: "Cain, where is your brother Abel?"

Adam and Eve had a third son, Seth, who became the ancestor of many tribes.

AGADAH

Great Is the Power of Repentance

When Cain went out from the presence of God, and wandered about aimlessly, all animals and beasts roared at him and threatened to devour him. They set their teeth against him and said: "Here is the man who murdered his brother. Come, let us tear him to pieces." Cain trembled with fright at their words, but the animals on approaching him beheld the mark that God had placed upon him, and dared not injure him.

One day Adam met Cain. He looked with wonder at the token of pardon on Cain's forehead, and asked: "My son, how did you turn away the wrath of the Almighty?"

"By confession and repentance," said Cain.

"Woe is me!" cried Adam, smiting his brow. "The virtue of repentance is so great, and I knew it not! To think that by repentance I might have altered my lot!"

QUESTIONS

1) Describe the dispositions of Cain and Abel.
2) Why was not God pleased with Cain's sacrifice?
3) What did God say to Cain when he failed to profit by Abel's example?
4) What was Cain's punishment?
5) What did a gentle voice whisper to Cain wherever he came?
6) Did Adam and Eve have another son, and what was his name?

———————

IV
THE GREAT FLOOD

Ten generations passed from the time Adam was created by the hand of God, and now there were many people inhabiting this world. But the people were bad. They forgot all about the good God in heaven, and they sinned and did wicked things. All creatures were corrupt, and God looked down with disdain upon them.

Of all the people that lived on earth at that time, only one righteous person could be found, a man whose name was Noah.

One day, God called to Noah and said: "Noah, I see that all the people on earth are extremely wicked; they rob and kill one another, and I must punish them for their wickedness. I will bring a great flood upon the earth, and all the wicked people will perish. But I will save you and your family because you are righteous. Now make for yourself an ark, and you and your family will go into the ark and be saved. With you in the ark you shall take in one pair of all unclean animals, and seven pairs of all clean animals, so that they, too, might be saved from death when I bring a flood."

Noah and his three sons, Shem, Ham and Japheth, and the rest of the family began building the ark. It was a hard task, but after a long time, the ark was completed.

Thereupon God said to Noah: "Now go and get together all the food you can find, and store it up in the ark, for you, for your family, and for the animals. Get all the animals and birds that are to be saved and bring them into the ark, for within seven days I shall bring a great flood of water upon the earth. Every living being that is not with you in the ark will perish."

Noah did as God had told him to do, and when he, and his family and all the animals were safe in the ark, it began to rain. It poured forty days and forty nights. The rain washed away the houses and everything that was in them. All the people and animals were drowned, but Noah and his family sailed safely on top of the water.

Weeks and months passed, and Noah opened the window of the ark. He sent out the raven, to see if it would find some dry place. The raven flew out of the window, but it did not find a dry spot. It flew to and fro, until the water dried up from the earth.

Noah waited seven more days, and he sent out a dove to see if the water has abated.

Noah Offered a Sacrifice to God

The dove flew and flew to look for dry land, but she could find no place where to rest her tired wings, and she came back to the ark. Noah put out his hand through the window, and he brought the dove back into the ark.

Seven days later, Noah again sent out the dove from the ark. This time the dove returned holding an olive leaf in her beak. Then Noah knew that the water was gradually drying up.

Noah waited seven more days, and he sent out the dove again. This time the dove did not come back, for she found dry land. Noah and his family then raised the roof of the ark and for the first time in many months, they again beheld the sweet sunshine, and what is more—dry land. The inhabitants of the ark now made ready to leave.

When Noah and his family came out of the ark, he offered a sacrifice to God for his deliverance. God thereupon said to Noah: "The man is evil from his youth, and I will no longer bring a flood to destroy mankind. As a token of my promise to you, I set my bow in the cloud. This will serve as a sign to all generations to come that I will no longer destroy all flesh by a flood."

AGADAH

A Foolish Shepherd

When Noah stepped out of the ark, he wept bitterly at the sight of the great destruction of life the flood had left in its train, and he said to God:

"O Lord of the World! You are called the Merciful, and you should have mercy upon your creatures."

"O you foolish shepherd;" replied God, "is it only now you bethink yourself to speak to me? When I told you that I would bring a flood to destroy all living things because of their wickedness, you then said nothing to me. But you were satisfied because you were assured of safety, and you did not concern yourself about the ruin the flood would bring. Now when you are saved, and the world lies waste at your feet, you beg for mercy."

Noah realized his error, and he brought an offering to God that his sin might be forgiven. God accepted his offering and blessed him.

QUESTIONS

1) Who was the only righteous man at that time?
2) What did God say to him, and why?
3) Whom was Noah to bring with him in the ark?
4) How was Noah saved from the flood?
5) How did Noah try to find out whether the flood was over?
6) What did the dove bring in her beak?
7) What was the promise that God had made to Noah?

V

THE FORMATION OF THE NATIONS

After many years, the human race once more became numerous. Families grew in number, and formed many distinct tribes. All the tribes lived peacefully side by side without strife, and all of them spoke the same language.

One day, the people were inspired with a bold plan. They said to one another: "Let us build a great city and a tower, whose top shall reach the sky, so that we may not be scattered over the whole earth."

So the people worked and worked, until they built a tower, which was already very high.

"It is not good for the people to stay all the time in one place," said God. "They must spread all over the earth and till the soil. Now, I am going to confuse their language, so that one should not be able to understand the language of the other."

The following day, the people awoke and came back to resume their work. They began to build the tower again, but they were taken by surprise. Everybody began to talk in a different language, and one was not able to understand the other. If one asked for bricks he was given water, and if one asked for water he was given cement. Thus they were forced to stop building the tower and were dispersed over the face of the earth. The city they had begun to build was called Babel (confusion), or Babylon.

From Babel, each little group went off in a different direction. Some went to the East, beyond the snowy mountains; some to the sunny South; some went to the icy North, and some to the West. Thereafter people lived as distinct tribes, each speaking its own language. They were all descendants of the three sons of Noah, Shem, Ham and Japheth. The tribes living in Western Asia, the Assyrians, the Elamites, the Arameans, the Hebrews and the Arabs, are called Semites, because they are the descendants of Shem. All the Asiatic and African tribes, the Egyptians, the Cushites, the Turanians, etc., are the descendants of Ham. The European peoples are the descendants of Japheth.

AGADAH
Brotherly Love

Nimrod, the mightiest hunter that ever lived, ascended the throne at that time. This mighty king said to his subjects: "Come, let us build a tower, the top of which shall reach the very heaven. God has taken for himself the heavens, and to us he gave the earth only. When we shall have built the tower, we shall be able to penetrate the heavens, fight God and put our own gods there. We will remain in the heavens until we become as mighty as God himself."

The people at once began to build the tower. Many, many years passed, and the tower reached a tremendous height. God looked down with disdain at the builders of the towers and said: "Verily, the people are extremely wicked, but I will not destroy them, because they love one another and live peacefully. I will simply confuse their language, so that they cease building the tower."

QUESTIONS

1) Why did the people build a high tower?
2) For what reason did not God want them to succeed?
3) By what means did God stop them from building it?
4) What is the meaning of *Babel?*
5) Whereto did the people go from Babel?
6) Why are the Hebrews called *Semites?*
7) Why did not God destroy the builders of the tower?

VI

THE MIGRATION OF ABRAHAM

In Ur, a city in Chaldea, there lived a certain man named Terah, a descendant of Shem. When well advanced in years, Terah took his family and migrated with them northwards to Haran, the land of the Arameans in Mesopotamia. Soon after he settled in Haran, Terah died at the age of two hundred and five years. One of the sons of Terah was Abram.

All the people who inhabited the globe at that time were idol-worshipers and believers in many gods; but Abram, the son of Terah, soon realized that the prevailing ideas were false. He founded the doctrine of the belief in one Supreme Being, God. One day, God appeared to Abram, and said to him: "Leave your own country and your father's house, and go to another land which I shall show you, for there a great people will spring from you."

Abram hearkened to the command of God, and, with his wife Sarai, his nephew Lot and his family, migrated to Canaan, or Palestine. In Canaan, Abram and his followers raised sheep and cattle.

They wandered about from place to place with their heards and flocks, pitching their tents wherever they found good pastureland.

Both, the family of Abram and the family of Lot, possessed great flocks, and the shepherds of the two families would often quarrel, because there was not sufficient pasture for both. One day, the good Abram said to his nephew Lot: "Pray let there be no quarrel between your shepherds and mine, for we are brothers. Behold, the whole country is open before us, then please let us separate. If you prefer to go to the left, then I will go to the right, and should you choose to go to the right, then I will go to the left."

Lot agreed to his uncle's suggestion, and he led his flocks and herdsmen in the direction of the Dead Sea on whose shores stood the city of Sodom. Abram pitched his tents near the city of Hebron in the plain of Mamre. In Canaan, Abram entered into a peaceful alliance with the chiefs of the Amorites. His allies looked upon Abram as the chief of a small nomadic tribe, whom they called *Hebrews,* which means *those who came from across the River (Euphrates).*

After Lot had left Abram, God appeared to the chief of the Hebrews and said to him: "Lift up your eyes, and look from the place where you are, northward, southward, eastward and westward; for all the land which you see I will give to you and to your children for ever."

AGADAH

Terah, the father of Abram, was a dealer in idols. One day, a woman came to Terah's house and said to Abram: "Here is some flour which I have brought for the gods. Please give it to them to eat."

As soon as the woman left the house, Abram took a hatchet and broke all the idols except the largest one of them which remained untouched. He then put the hatchet into the hand of the largest idol and left the room.

Shortly after Terah returned home and he was extremely angry upon seeing all his idols broken into pieces. He called in Abram and inquired in a very harsh voice: "Why have you broken all my idols?"

"Father, I did not do that," replied Abram. "It was the largest god who shattered all the rest, and this is how it came about. A certain woman came and brought a meat-offering to your gods, and I set it before them to eat. The gods began to quarrel among themselves, each one wanting to get it first. Their behavior angered the biggest god, so he took a hatchet and killed them all. There, you can still see him standing there holding the hatchet in his hand. And if you will not believe my words, ask him, and he will tell you."

"You speak lies to me!" exclaimed Terah in great fury. "These gods can neither eat nor drink nor do anything. Are they not mere wood and stone? And have I not myself made them? They cannot do the things you speak of. It is you who broke them and you who placed the hatchet in the hand of the big idol."

Abram who had expected just such an answer, joyfully exclaimed: "True, father, the idols are nothing but mere wood and stone, the work of your hands. But how then, O father, can you worship these gods, who possess no power to do anything. Can these pieces of wood and stone deliver you from your troubles. Can they hear your prayers?" And after having spoken these words, Abram took the hatchet from the big god and smashed it, too.

———————

QUESTIONS

1) What was the name of Abram's father, and where did he live?
2) What did people believe in those days, and what doctrine did Abram found?
3) Whom did Abram take along when he migrated to Canaan?
4) Why did the shepherds of Abram and Lot quarrel?
5) What did Abram then say to Lot?
6) Why was Abram called by the Natives *Hebrew?*

VII
THE WAR WITH THE BABYLONIANS

In those days the Babylonians were the rulers of Asia. Sodom and the kings of four other countries on the coast of the Dead Sea, were vassals of the mighty kings of Elam and Babylonia.

Once these vassal kings decided to cast off the yoke of their rulers, and they rebelled against the kings of Elam and Babylonia. The mighty ruling kings brought their armies from Elam and Babylonia and invaded the land of Canaan to crush the rebels. They plundered the city of Sodom and the neighboring kingdoms, carried off a great deal of booty, and took many of their people into captivity.

The victorious kings took also Abram's nephew Lot as captive, and confiscated all his property. An escaped captive came to Abram and informed him of the sad plight of his nephew. Abram immediately armed his three hundred and eighteen faithful servants, summoned the aid of the three chieftains with whom he had made a treaty of peace, and went in pursuit of the invaders. He surprised the victorious kings in a night attack, thoroughly defeated them, and took from them all the captives and the booty.

When Abram returned from his successful adventure, he was met by the king of Sodom who said: "Abram, you may keep all the booty for yourself as a reward, but return to me the prisoners of war."

But Abram replied: "I swear by the Lord, God Most High, Creator of heaven and earth, that not one thread or shoestring will I take from you, lest you say: 'I have made Abram rich'."

Abram soon became famous throughout the land of Canaan for his valor and wealth. Moreover, Abram and his wife Sarai were very kind and helpful to the poor and needy of the land. Abram would sit daily at the entrance of his large tent to invite every traveler to enter and refresh himself. Abram and his good wife were therefore loved by all the inhabitants of Canaan.

After this incident, God appeared to Abram and said to him: "Fear not, Abram, for I am a shield to you." God then took Abram outside and added: "Your children shall be as numerous as the stars of heaven." Thereupon God made a covenant with Abram, and when the sun was about to set, a deep sleep fell upon Abram, and the voice of God addressed him: "Know that for four hundred

years your offspring shall be in a foreign land,
where they will be oppressed. But I shall judge
their oppressors, and your children shall depart
from there with great riches. Then I will give to
your children this land, from the Nile to the Euphrates."

Thereafter, when God appeared again to Abram, he said to him: Your name shall henceforth
be, not *Abram,* but *Abraham* (meaning the *father
of a multitude*). And your wife's name shall henceforth be, not *Sarai,* but *Sarah* (meaning *queen*)."

AGADAH

"The Shield of Abraham"

The kings that were defeated by Abraham
gathered in the valley of Shove, and asked Abraham to become their king and god. But Abraham
replied: "God forbid that I shall be your king,
much less your god, for I am but a mortal like any
one of you. If you desire to reward me, I would
ask you to love one another, live in peace, and open
wide the doors of your tents for the needy, the suffering and the wayfarer. Pray to the God in
heaven, the Creator of heaven and earth, and serve
him with all your heart. For it is not with the
power of my hands that I have succeeded in this
battle. It is the God in heaven that was my shield."

Thereupon the sweet voices of angels were heard in heaven chanting a prayer to God: "Blessed are you, O Lord, the shield of Abraham."

QUESTIONS

1) Who made war against Sodom, and why?
2) How did Abraham know that Lot was taken captive?
3) What did Abraham do when he received the news?
4) What offer did the king of Sodom make to Abraham?
5) What did Abraham reply?
6) Relate the details of Abraham's vision.
7) What is the meaning of *Abraham?*
8) What is the meaning of *Sarah?*

VIII
THE VISIT OF THE ANGELS

One day, Abraham was sitting at the entrance of his tent, because the day was extremely hot. While sitting there he noticed three weary wayfarers coming towards him along the road. Abraham, although already an old man, for he was then one hundred years old, ran to meet the strangers, and he pleaded: "O please, gentlemen, the day is so hot, and you are tired and weary. Pray enter my tent, where you can rest and eat."

The strangers accepted Abraham's invitation, and they sat down under the shade of a tree that grew near Abraham's tent. Abraham at once ran to the tent of his wife Sarah and said to her: "Pray, good wife, prepare some food quickly, for three tired, hungry men have come to our tent."

Abraham himself brought a bucketful of fresh water for the strangers to wash their tired feet. Through with that he ran to the herd, picked out a tender young kid, and prepared delicious meat for the guests. The strangers ate the meal, and Abraham stood beside them all the time, ready to serve them.

When the strangers had eaten, one of them turned to Abraham and said: "Kind host, know you that your good wife Sarah will embrace a son of her own next year at this time."

Abraham Pleaded With the Strangers

Sarah, who then happened to stand at the entrance of her tent, overheard the words of the stranger, and she laughed within herself, saying: "My husband is one hundred years old, and I am ninety years. Shall I now give birth to a child?"

The angel who could read Sarah's thoughts, rebuked her for this, and said: "Is there anything too hard for the Lord?" Then the strangers set out toward Sodom, and Abraham accompanied them on the way.

AGADAH
Hospitality

Abraham, always ready and anxious to give shelter and food to wayfarers, made a tent with doors opening on all sides, so that they might enter it, no matter from which direction they came, and eat of his bread.

One day, Abraham was very sick and was unable to wait upon strangers. God therefore took out the sun from its sheath, and made the day so hot that no one ventured go out of the house. "My servant Abraham is sick," said God, "let no stranger enter his tent and disturb him."

Abraham, accustomed to receive strangers, was greatly vexed when he saw that none came to his tent. He called for his servant Eliezer, and said to him: "I am sick and unable to leave my tent. Pray go outside, look around and see if you can find any wayfarers. If you see a stranger pass by, invite him into our tent where he can refresh himself and rest from his wearisome journey."

Eliezer bowed and departed to comply with his master's request. He looked around in every direction and seeing no one come, he returned and said: "Master, I saw no one pass by."

Abraham, in spite of his illness and the scorching heat, went outside and looked east, north, west, and south, and when he saw no one passing, he was extremely grieved. He said to himself: "Perhaps there are some wayfarers traveling in the desert who are tortured by the scorching sun and are unable to find shelter."

When God saw the anxiety of his servant Abraham, he sent down to him three angels in the form of human beings. They were the angels Michael, Gabriel, and Raphael. Raphael was sent down to cure Abraham of his sickness, Michael was to bring Sarah the glad news that by next year a son would be born to her, and Gabriel was to destroy the wicked cities of Sodom and Gomorrah.

QUESTIONS

1) What did Abraham do when he saw the three strangers?
2) What did Abraham say to Sarah?
3) What did Abraham himself do?
4) How old was he then?
5) What did one of the strangers say to Abraham?
6) Where was Sarah at that time, and what did she do?
7) What did the angel say to Abraham then?
8) Where did the angels go to after that?

IX

THE DESTRUCTION OF SODOM

Now, the people of Sodom and of the other cities on the shores of the Dead Sea were extremely wicked and cruel. God revealed to Abraham that a great calamity was about to overtake the sinful inhabitants of Sodom and of the neighboring cities. But Abraham implored God to spare the Sodomites, saying: "O Lord, will you destroy the righteous together with the wicked? Perhaps there are fifty good men within the city; will you nevertheless destroy the whole city and spare it not for the sake of the fifty good men that are there?"

God replied: "If I find in Sodom fifty righteous men, I will spare the whole city for their sake."

"Supposing there will be found only forty-five righteous men in Sodom," said Abraham, "will you destroy the cities, because there are five righteous men wanting of the fifty?"

"No," replied God again, "if I find forty-five righteous men there, I will spare the whole city for their sake."

Then Abraham begged for mercy again and again, and asked God to spare the inhabitants of Sodom for the sake of a smaller and smaller number of righteous men. Finally Abraham pleaded: "Supposing you find only ten righteous men in Sodom, will you then, O Lord, destroy the city?"

"No," said the merciful God, "even if I find only ten righteous men in Sodom, I will spare the whole city for their sake."

But so great was the corruption of the citizens of Sodom and its neighbors, that not even ten righteous men could be found among them. Two of the angels that enjoyed Abraham's hospitality now betook themselves to Sodom. One of them was to destroy the sinful cities, and the other was to save Abraham's nephew Lot, his wife and his two daughters, from the doomed city.

When the two angels reached Sodom the sun was about to set. Lot who had learned from his uncle Abraham to be hospitable to strangers, invited the angels to stay in his house over night. The angels accepted the invitation, but before they lay down to rest, the wicked people of Sodom surrounded Lot's house with the intention of doing harm to them. Lot pleaded with the people to be merciful this once, but in vain. The angels now pulled Lot into the house, and smote the men outside with blindness, so that they were unable to find the entrance to the tent.

The angels then told Lot that they would destroy the sinful city the next day. They therefore urged him to leave the city early in the morning, together with his wife and his two daughters. In the morning, when Lot and his family were at a safe distance from the city, torrents of fire and brimstone fell from the heavens upon Sodom, Gomorrah and the other cities of wickedness. Everything was destroyed in the flames, the people perished, and the country became a dismal wilderness beside the borders of the Dead Sea.

While taking Lot and his family out of Sodom, the angel said to them: "You may escape to that place yonder, but when you flee you must not turn around to see what is going on behind you. If you do turn around to look, you will die."

But Lot's wife disobeyed the command of the angel, and she did turn around to look as she fled. God punished her for that, and she was turned into a pillar of salt.

Lot and his family went to live in the mountains. There a son was born to each of Lot's daughters. The son of the elder daughter was named Moab, who later became the chief of the Moabite tribe. The son of the younger daughter was named

Ben-Ami, who became the founder of the Ammonite tribe. In after years, these tribes formed two separate kingdoms on the eastern banks of the Jordan.

AGADAH

A Girl Stung to Death by Bees

The people of Sodom and of the neighboring cities were very rich, because their land was fertile, and in the ground were found treasures of silver, gold, and precious stones. But the richer the Sodomites grew the more wicked they became. They permitted no strangers to enter their cities, and if any one happened to come there, they would let him starve to death.

One day, a wayfarer came into Sodom and sat down in one of the streets of the city to rest, for no one would give him any shelter. In the middle of the night, one of the maidens of the city happened to pass by the stranger, and she said to him: "Where do you come from, and whither are you going?"

"I come from a very distant city," replied the stranger, "and when I arrived to Sodom the sun had already set. I will merely stay here over night, and in the early morning I shall continue my journey. Come, dear maiden," he pleaded, "give me some water, because my tongue is parched with thirst. Pray have pity on me."

Moved by the plea of the stranger, the kind hearted maiden hurried home and fetched for him some bread and water. After the man had eaten and drunk, he blessed the maiden in the name of God. When the merciless, cruel judges of Sodom became aware that the girl dared have pity on a stranger, they placed her on trial. The judges sentenced the maiden to death, and the wicked people of Sodom invented a scheme to torture the poor girl to death for her kindness. They smeared her body with honey from the crown of her head to the tip of her toe, and placed her near beehives. Numerous bees at once began buzzing around her in great swarms, and stung the kind maiden to death.

The victim uttered one shrill cry of agony, which ascended to heaven and reached Almighty God. Thereupon God said to the angels: "This cry moves me to action. Descend to earth and put an end to the evil deeds of the Sodomites."

QUESTIONS

1) Where were Sodom and the other sinful cities situated?
2) For the sake of how many people did Abraham plead that God save the sinful cities?
3) Whereto did two of the angels that had been in Abraham's house go?
4) Whom did the angels want to save from the doomed cities?
5) Why was Lot's wife turned into a pillar of salt?
6) What were the two kingdoms that descended from Lot?

X

ISHMAEL AND ISAAC

Besides his beloved wife Sarah, Abraham had another wife named Hagar, who had been one of his Egyptian slaves. She bore him a son, who was named Ishmael, but Ishmael was not destined to become Abraham's successor as the chief of the Hebrew tribe.

The prediction of the angel came true, and within a year Sarah bore a son who received the name of Isaac. At God's command, Isaac was circumcised at the age of eight days, and Ishmael was circumcised at the age of thirteen years. Ever since that time the custom of circumcision has become a fixed practice mong both the Hebrews and the Arabs (Ishmaelites).

Isaac's half-brother, Ishmael grew up to be a very wild boy. He liked to go out hunting all the time, and he was fond of fighting. Even little Isaac he did not spare. Ishmael's conduct displeased Isaac's mother Sarah, and she one day begged Abraham to send away both Ishmael and his mother Hagar. The kind heart of Abraham was very grieved, for he was unwilling to thus hurt his son and his wife, but God appeared to Abraham and said: "Do whatever Sarah tells you to do."

So Abraham, with a reluctant heart, sent away Hagar and her son, supplying them with bread and water to sustain them in their wanderings.

Abraham Sent Away Hagar and Her Son

Then Hagar went into the desert where she lost her way. The water soon gave out, and the two lonely wanderers had nothing to drink. The boy was parched with thirst, and he was at last too weak and tired to walk any further. Shedding bitter tears, Hagar put the boy under the shade of some shrubs, and sat down a little way off, for she said: "Let my eyes not see my child die of thirst!"

But Ishmael was not to die. As the grief-stricken mother sat there and wept, she heard the voice of God's messenger calling to her: "What troubles you, Hagar? Fear not; for God has heard the voice of the lad. Arise, lift him up, and hold fast by his hand; for I will make of him a great nation."

As Hagar turned around, she suddenly beheld a well of water right by her side. Joyfully she filled her skin bottle with water, and gave the boy to drink. Ishmael had a good drink, and he soon felt better. After a long journey, Hagar and Ishmael came to the wilderness of Paran, and there they remained. Ishmael grew up to be a very strong and healthy man, and he became a skilled bowman. His descendants lived the life of nomads in the Arabian desert south of Palestine, and he is known as the father of the Arabs.

AGADAH
No One Is Punished for the Future

God heard the cries of Ishmael, and he was about to make a spring of water come out for him so that he be saved from death. The angels thereupon said: "O Merciful God! Why would you have mercy upon Ishmael and save him from death? Surely it is known to you that in days to come his descendants will cause the children of Israel, your chosen people, to perish from thirst, when they shall be exiled from their land."

"Tell me," said God to the angels, "what is Ishmael at present, righteous or wicked?"

"He is righteous at present," replied they, "for he is yet unable to differentiate between right and wrong."

"Know you, therefore," stated the merciful God, "that I do not judge men by the acts that they will do in the future, but by the acts they are doing at the present time."

QUESTIONS

1) How many sons did Abraham have, and what were their names?
2) Why did the conduct of Ishmael displease Sarah?
3) Was Abraham willing to do Sarah's request? Why then did he do it?
4) What happened to Ishmael and Hagar in the Wilderness?
5) How was Ishmael saved from death?
6) Who are the descendants of Ishmael?

XI
THE TRIAL OF ABRAHAM

Though Abraham lived among heathens and idol-worshipers, he remained loyal to the belief in one Supreme Being, the Creator of the world.

There came a day when God put Abraham's loyalty to the test, so he said to Abraham: "Take your son, your only son, whom you love, even Isaac, and go to the land of Moriah; and offer him there as a burnt-offering upon one of the mountains which I will show you."

Abraham loved Isaac dearly, and would have gladly given up his own life to spare his son, but he dared not disobey the will of God. He made no reply to the command of God, but he rose early in the morning, saddled his donkey, cut some wood which he tied in a bundle, and fastened it on Isaac's back. He took a big knife with him, and he also took something with which to start a fire. Abraham, his son Isaac, and two of his servants then started on their journey to the mountain of Moriah.

53

At the end of three days, Abraham and his party came to the foot of the mountain. Abraham then said to his two servants: "You remain here at the foot of the mountain, but my son and I will go yonder to the top of the mountain where we will worship God and then return to you."

As Isaac trudged along by his father's side, he asked: "Father, I see the wood, and a knife, and fire, but where is the lamb for the sacrifice?"

"Oh," said Abraham, his voice almost choking with tears, "God will provide the sacrifice, my son."

Abraham and Isaac at last reached the top of the mountain. Abraham now put some stones together, and laid the wood on it. He then turned to his son and said: "My dear son, God told me not to sacrifice a little lamb, but he ordered me to sacrifice you as an offering to him."

Isaac made no reply. Neither did he protest or cry when Abraham, his good, dear father, tied his hands and feet and put him on the wood piled up on the stones.

Abraham raised his long sharp knife, ready to cut the outstretched neck of his beloved son, when the voice of God was heard from heaven, saying: "Lay not your hand upon the lad, neither do you anything to him: for now I know that you are a

God-fearing man, that you have not withheld your son, your only one, from me."

Abraham then looked about him and saw a ram whose horns were entangled in the branches of a bush. Overjoyed, the father unbound his son, and offered the ram as a burnt-offering instead of his son. Abraham again heard the voice of an angel say to him: "By myself have I sworn," says the Lord, "because you have done this thing, and have not withheld your son, your only son, from me, that I will bless you and will multiply your children as the stars of the heaven, and as the sand which is upon the sea-shore; and in your children shall all the nations of the earth be blessed."

AGADAH

A Kind Father and a Thoughtful Son

The only thing that troubled Isaac when he was placed upon the wood by his father was the thought of his dear mother. Isaac then implored: "Pray, father, do not inform my mother of my death while she is standing on the roof, lest she throw herself down in her despair. Do not inform my mother of my death while she is passing a well, lest she throw herself into it. Burn my body into fine ashes, gather them into a casket and place it in my mother's chamber. At all hours, when she enters the chamber, she will remember her son Isaac and weep for him."

Having received no reply from his father, Isaac continued: "And my father, what will you and my mother do in your old age? Who will bring you consolation in time of grief?"

"We can survive you by a few days only," answered the very unhappy father; "and he who was our comfort before you were born, will comfort us henceforth."

When Abraham was ordered by God not to slay his son, he said: "Almighty God, I will not leave this altar until I have said what I have to say." God gave him permission to speak, and Abraham continued: "When you have commanded me to sacrifice my son Isaac, I could have argued with you: 'O Lord, yesterday you told me: "In Isaac shall your children be called," and now you tell me to offer him as a burnt-offering to you; how then can your former promise be fulfilled?' But I said nothing. I was ready and willing to perform your command and offer my son to you, although he is much dearer to me than my own life. I therefore pray to you, O merciful God, that when my children in generations to come will arouse your anger by sinning against you, you shall forgive them and deliver them from their suffering."

God replied: "When I shall sit in judgment upon your children on New Year's day, I will grant them pardon if they blow the ram's horn on that day. For that will remind me of the ram that was substituted by you as a sacrifice in the stead of Isaac."

QUESTIONS

1) How did God try Abraham's faith in him?
2) In what place was Abraham told to take Isaac?
3) What did Abraham take along with him?
4) What did Isaac ask of his father?
5) And what was the reply given him?
6) Why did Abraham abstain from killing his son?
7) What did he sacrifice instead of Isaac?

XII
DEATH OF SARAH

Sarah, the mother of the Hebrews, died at the age of one hundred and twenty-seven years. Abraham was a nomad, a wandering shepherd, and as such possessed no land of his own. Abraham possessed not even a place in which to bury his wife. Approaching the children of Heth, a tribe in the land of Canaan, Abraham said to them: "I am a stranger among you; pray give me a piece of land where I may bury my wife Sarah."

Now, Abraham, the chief of the small Hebrew tribe, was very much beloved by the people for his kindness and his heroism, and the sons of Heth said to him: "Our lord, you are a mighty prince among us; in the choice of our graveyards you may bury your dead; none of us shall withold his graveyard from you."

Abraham bowed to the people in recognition of their friendship to him, and he said to them: "If you are so kind to me, pray ask Ephron, the son of Zohar, that he give me the Cave of Machpelah, which is in his field; and I will pay for it the full price."

Thereupon Ephron, the son of Zohar, offered to
give Abraham the Cave of Machpelah as a gift,
but Abraham courteously but firmly declined his

Abraham Approaching the Children of Heth

kindness, and paid him the sum of four hundred
silver shekels for it. Thus the Cave of Machpelah,
situated in Hebron, together with the land sur-
rounding it, became the property of Abraham, the
chief of the Hebrews. There Sarah, the mother
of the Hebrews, was laid to rest.

AGADAH

Abraham Withstands Another Temptation

Sarah was very much grieved over the safety of her only son Isaac, and, old and feeble as she was, she left her tent in search of her son. She wandered and wandered, asking of all whom she met: "Did you, good people, perchance happen to see my son Isaac?"

None of the passers-by seemed to know anything about Isaac, and Sarah kept on wandering in search of her son, until she reached Hebron. There the pious mother of the Hebrews passed out in grief and worry over her son.

Abraham and Isaac, upon their returning from the land of Moriah, were not a little surprised to find the door of Sarah's tent locked; they also noticed that the light that used to continually burn in her tent, was now put out. They ran to their neighbors to find out the cause of it all.

"Oh," said the neighbors, "Sarah went in the direction of Hebron in search of Isaac." Abraham and Isaac at once betook themselves to Hebron, and to their great grief they found Sarah dead.

Now God had promised to give the whole land of Canaan to Abraham and to his children, and yet Abraham did not possess even as much as a grave to bury his wife. Still Abraham did not complain to God; he firmly believed that in time to come God's promise will be fulfilled.

QUESTIONS

1) At what age did Sarah die?
2) Who offered to give Abraham the choice of their burial-places?
3) What did Ephron offer to give to Abraham?
4) Did Abraham accept the offer?
5) How much did Abraham pay for the cave?
6) Where is the cave situated?

XIII
REBECCA. DEATH OF ABRAHAM

When Abraham was far advanced in years and Isaac grew to manhood, the aged father felt that it was time to choose a wife for his son. Calling Eliezer, his devoted servant, to his side, he said to him: "Swear to me that you will not take a wife for my son of the daughters of the Canaanites among whom I dwell. But you shall go to my country Mesopotamia, and from there bring a wife for my son Isaac.

Eliezer took with him a number of servants and ten camels laden with provisions for the way and started on his mission. When he reached the place of his destination, the sun was about to set and the maidens of the town were about to come out to the well to draw water. As he waited for their coming, Eliezer prayed thus: "O God of my master Abraham, show kindness to my master and cause my mission to be terminated according to his desire. Here I stand by the well, and the maidens will soon come out to draw water. Let this be the sign as to whom you have designated to be Isaac's wife. If I ask one of them for a drink, and she draws water not only for me but for my camels also, then I shall know that she is the one who is destined to be the wife of Isaac." ~

Eliezer and Rebecca

As soon as Eliezer finished praying, a maiden appeared carrying a pitcher on her shoulder, and after she filled her pitcher, Eliezer hastened towards her and said: "Please, give me a drink from your pitcher."

Promptly the maiden lifted the pitcher from her shoulder to let Eliezer drink. When he had his fill, she said: "Your camels seem to be thirsty; I will draw water for your camels also, until they have done drinking."

She emptied her pitcher into the trough, and ran to the well to draw water again, and thus she kept on drawing water for all the camels. Eliezer was amazed at the kindness and the beauty of the maiden, and he presented her with golden ear-rings and two bracelets. Then he said to her: "Tell me, pray, whose daughter you are. Is there any room for us in your father's house to stay over night?"

The maiden replied: "I am Rebecca, the daughter of Bethuel and granddaughter of Nahor, Abraham's brother. We have room for you to stay over night, and we also have straw and provender for your camels."

Rebecca hastened home and told her mother what had happened. Her brother Laban went out to meet Eliezer and brought him to his parents' house. Eliezer was requested to partake of food, but he said: "I shall taste no food before I have told my mission." He then told them of his master's request, and also of the sign he had agreed upon when he came to the well. Then Rebecca's kinsmen replied: "It was the will of God that Rebecca should become the wife of Isaac. There stands Rebecca before you; let us ask her if she consents to go with you to your master's house." When Rebecca gave her consent, the maiden's kinsmen said: "Take her with you and let her become the wife of your master's son."

Eliezer presented Rebecca and her relatives with rich gifts, and on the following morning, Rebecca's kinsmen gave her their blessing and allowed her to go with Eliezer to Canaan.

Abraham lived for some years after Isaac's marriage to Rebecca. He died at the age of one hundred and seventy-five years, and he was buried by his sons Ishmael and Isaac beside Sarah in the Cave of Machpelah near Hebron.

AGADAH

1. *The Kind Rebecca*

When Rebecca came to the well and drew some water in her pitcher, she saw a little boy crying nearby. She approached him and inquired: "What happened to you, little boy?"

"I hit my foot against a stone, and now it is bleeding," answered the boy, scared at the sight of blood. Rebecca immediately took her pitcher off her shoulder and washed the boys' wounded foot. She also took off her kerchief and dressed the wound with it. "Now," she said to the boy, "you may return home, and do not worry, for you will soon be cured."

When she walked a little further, she met a blind woman to whom she said: "Pray tell me, do you know your way home?"

"If I do not find my way home," the blind woman replied, "I will stay in the open field over night as I did the night before."

"Do tell me where you live," persisted Rebecca, "so that I can lead you home." The woman thanked her, and Rebecca took her to her house.

When Rebecca returned to the well, she was tired, and as she sat down on a stump of a tree to rest, an old man happened to pass by. She at once jumped to her feet and said to the old man: "You look tired; sit upon the stump and rest yourself." The old man thanked Rebecca for her kindness and sat down to rest. The kind maiden then went to the well again, and filled her pitcher.

All this time Eliezer closely watched Rebecca's actions, and he thought: "Surely this kind maiden is worthy to become the wife of my master's son."

2. *Everybody Mourns the Loss*

When the death of Abraham became known, everybody mourned the great loss. And thus did all the great men of the nations of the world say: "Woe to the world whose leader is gone, woe to the ship whose helmsman is gone."

QUESTIONS

1) What did Abraham request of Eliezer?
2) How was Eliezer to know who was to become the wife of Isaac?
3) Who was the maiden that satisfied Eliezer's wish?
4) How was she related to Isaac?
5). What did Rebecca's kinsmen say to Eliezer?
6) How old was Abraham when he died?
7) Where was he buried?

XIV
SALE OF THE BIRTHRIGHT

The life of Isaac was uneventful. On the whole he lived a peaceful life, and always avoided strife. He continued to walk in the footsteps of his pious father Abraham, and spread the belief in one Supreme Being. God repeated the promise to Isaac that his children would be numerous, that his children would be given the promised land, and that through them all the nations of the earth would be blessed.

Isaac was a farmer, and he had very successful harvests. He became rich, and his neighbors grew jealous of him. Isaac would work hard with his men to dig wells, and the neighboring people, called Philistines, would take them away from him. At times the jealous neighbors would choke up the wells with earth just for spite. Now, water in the East is very scarce, and a spring of water is a very valuable thing, but Isaac would not fight with his jealous neighbors. He would give up one well after another rather than fight about them.

At last the jealous neighbors began to admire Isaac's patience and character. They came to Isaac and asked him to forgive them and to be friends with them.   So they made an agreement of peace.

Isaac was forty years when he married Rebecca. She bore him twin sons, Esau and Jacob.   When the boys grew up, Esau became fond of hunting wild animals, and he was therefore called "a man of the field," but Jacob preferred the peaceful life of a shepherd and he was known as "a tent-dweller."

One day, while Jacob sat in his tent eating a pottage of lentils which he had prepared for himself, Esau entered.   Esau had just returned from hunting, and he was tired and hungry.   Esau said to his brother: "Let me have some of this red pottage."

Now, Esau was the older of the twins and, according to the Hebrew custom, he would become the chief of the Hebrew tribe after the death of Isaac.   Jacob thereupon said to Esau: "Sell me your birthright, and I will give you for it some pottage of lentils."

"Behold I shall die," said Esau, "and what good is the birthright to me?"

Then Esau gave up his birthright to Jacob in return for some bread and pottage of lentils. Isaac, however, still regarded Esau as the elder son. Esau was his favorite, for he would very often bring home with him some game he had killed, prepare it himself, and offer it to his father. But the gentle Jacob was the more beloved of his mother Rebecca.

AGADAH

Esau Makes Sport of the Birthright

When Esau entered the tent, he said to Jacob: "Why are you preparing lentils today?"

"Because our grandfather Abraham passed away," Jacob replied, "and these lentils are used by me as a mourner's meal."

"If the pious as well as the wicked die," exclaimed Esau, "what good is it to be righteous and pious? Now we can see that there is no special reward for the righteous. Why then should I exert myself to do what is good? Come Jacob, let me have some of the lentils, for I am tired and hungry."

"Why should an un-believer enjoy the birthright?" argued Jacob to himself. Then facing his brother, he said to him: "Tell me, brother, if you do not believe in the hereafter, and that God will reward the righteous and punish the wicked, will you sell me the birthright for the lentils which I am to give you."

"Oh, I am going to die anyway," said Esau, "and what good is the birthright to me? You can have it; but let me have some of your wine, lentils and bread."

When Esau finished his meal, he invited his friends to come and make game of Jacob. "Now see, my friends," said Esau to them, "what I did to Jacob. I ate his lentils, drank his wine, and sold my birthright to him." Jacob did not reply to his brother's jeers, but said: "Swear to me by the life of our father that you sell me the birthright." Esau did so, and he even signed a document in which he gave up all his rights to the Cave of Machpelah.

QUESTIONS

1) What was Isaac's occupation?
2) Why were the neighbors jealous of Isaac?
3) What did the neighbors do?
4) Describe the characters of Esau and Jacob.
5) Tell how Jacob got the birthright.
6) Whom did Isaac love, and whom did Rebecca love?

XV
JACOB RECEIVES THE BLESSING

When Jacob grew very old, and his eyes were dim so that he was unable to see, he called Esau to him one day, and said: "My son, I am very old, and I do not know the day of my death. Take your weapons, and go out to the field, hunt some game, prepare it for me in the manner I love, and bring it to me. Then I will bless you before I die."

Rebecca overheard what Isaac said to Esau. She was unwilling that Isaac's blessing be given to Esau instead of to her favorite son Jacob. She therefore called Jacob to her and told him of the conversation she had overheard between Isaac and Esau. Then she added: "Now, my son, listen to what I command you. Go to the flock at once and fetch me two good kids. I will prepare of them savory food, such as your father likes. Then you shall bring the food to your father, so that he may bless you before his death."

Now, the body of Esau was hairy, while the body of Jacob was smooth. And Jacob said to his mother: "If my father will feel me and find that my skin is smooth, I shall seem to him a deceiver, and bring a curse upon me instead of a blessing."

Rebecca replied: "Upon me be the curse, my son. Only hearken to my voice, and go fetch me the two kids."

Jacob obeyed his mother. He went to the herd, killed two delicate kids, and brought them to his mother. Rebecca at once prepared from their flesh Isaac's favorite dish. She then dressed Jacob in Esau's hunting clothes, and wrapped his neck and hands with the skins of the kids. Jacob carried the food to his father and said: "I am your first-born son; I prepared the food for you as you bade me. Now please rise, eat of the food, and give me your blessing."

Isaac recognized Jacob's voice, and he said: "Come near me, my son, that I may feel you to make sure you are my very son Esau."

Jacob approached his father, who felt him and said: "The voice is the voice of Jacob, but the hands are the hands of Esau."

Isaac thereupon blessed Jacob with the words:

"May God give you of the dew of heaven,
And of the fat places of the earth,
And plenty of corn and wine.
Let people serve you,
And nations bow down to you.

Be lord over your brethren,
And let your mother's sons bow down to you.
Cursed be everyone that curses you,
And blessed be everyone that blesses you."

Isaac Blessed Jacob

No sooner had Jacob left the tent of his father than Esau returned from the field. He too prepared some venison which he brought to his father, and said: "I am your first-born son Esau. Arise, father, and eat of the venison I have prepared for you, that you may bless me."

Isaac trembled and said: "Who then is he that

has brought venison to me before you came, and whom I have blessed? Yea, and he shall be blessed."

Esau cried bitterly, for he understood that Jacob had outwitted him, and he said to his father: "Father, have you only one blessing to give? Bless me also!"

Isaac blessed his favorite son with the words:

"Behold, of the fat places of the earth shall
   be your dwelling,
And of the dew of heaven from above;
And by your sword shall you live."

AGADAH

Jacob Is Rewarded for His Gentleness
When Jacob entered the tent of his father with the food and spoke to his father in gentle words, a voice came down from heaven saying: "Because Jacob spoke so softly and gently to his father, I will help his children in time of distress, and disperse all their enemies."

QUESTIONS

1) Whom did Isaac want to bless, and why?
2) Who overheard the conversation, and what did she do?
3) What did Jacob say to his mother, and what was her reply?
4) Why did Rebecca cover the neck and hands of Jacob with the skins of the kids?
5) Tell what took place between Isaac and Jacob.
6) When did Esau come in, and what happened after that?

XVI
JACOB FLEES TO MESOPOTAMIA

From that day on, Esau hated his brother Jacob, and he made up his mind to kill him as soon as their father died. Rebecca, who became aware of Esau's intentions, called Jacob to her and said: "Your brother Esau intends to take your life. Now therefore, my son, hearken to my words, and flee to my brother Laban who is in Haran, and stay with him there until your brother's anger will be appeased."

At the request of Rebecca, Isaac told Jacob to go to Mesopotamia, and there take to wife one of the daughters of Laban. Isaac gave Jacob his blessing, and Jacob, all by himself, set out upon his long journey.

It was a dreary journey from Canaan to Mesopotamia, and Jacob did not have even a camel to ride upon. He was tired and weary when night overtook him. With no dwelling in sight, Jacob was obliged to sleep out in the open with no shelter, and with only a stone under his head. As his eyes closed and he fell asleep, everything about him seemed to change; it was no longer the dreary, lonely spot.

Jacob had a wonderful dream. He saw before him a ladder standing upright, and the top of it reached up to heaven. Upon this heavenly staircase angels were ascending and descending. Then Jacob heard the voice of God saying to him: "I am the Lord, the God of Abraham your father, and the God of Isaac. The land whereon you lie, I will give to you and to your children; and you shall spread abroad to the west, to the east, to the north and to the south. In you and in your children all the families of the earth shall be blessed. Behold, I am with you, and will keep you withersoever you go, and will bring you back into this land."

Jacob awoke out of his sleep with a start, and he said: "Surely the Lord is in this place, and I knew it not. This is none other than the house of God, and this is the gate of heaven."

Jacob rose early in the morning, and he took the stone upon which he had slept and set it up as a monument. He called the name of the place Bethel, a House of God.

As Jacob walked on, he came across some flocks of sheep, lying about a well. Jacob asked the shepherds why they did not water their flocks, so that they might pasture again in the meadows. The shepherds replied that a big rock covered the mouth of the well, and that they were therefore compelled to wait until all the shepherds would come so that together they might roll off the rock from the well.

Jacob then asked them if they knew Laban, and the shepherds replied that they knew him. While they were thus talking, one of the shepherds said: "Here comes Rachel, the daughter of Laban, with her flock."

When Jacob saw Rachel, the daughter of his uncle, he went up to the well, and he himself rolled off the great stone from the mouth of the well, and watered the flock of his uncle. Jacob then told Rachel that he was her cousin, the son of her aunt Rebecca who was living in Canaan. Rachel hastened home and informed her father of the visitor that had arrived from Canaan. Laban in turn hastened to the well, welcomed his nephew and took him to his home.

AGADAH
The Vision

Jacob in his dream saw the angels of the four kingdoms, Babylon, Media, Greece and Edom ascending the ladder. The angel of Babylon mounted seventy rundles, the angel of Media fifty-two, the angel of Greece, one hundred and eighty; and the angel of Edom mounted very high, and failed to descend.

Jacob was very much dissappointed and said: "O Lord, shall this angel forever remain on high, and my children shall remain in exile in his land never to be redeemed?" Thereupon Jacob heard the voice of God saying: "Though he mount on high as the eagle, and though his nest be set among the stars, I will bring him down from thence."

God then folded together the whole land of Palestine, put it under Jacob and said to him: "The land upon which you are lying to you will I give it and to your children. And your children," the promise continued, "shall be like the dust of the earth. As the earth survives all things, so will your children survive all the nations of the earth. But as the earth is trodden upon by all, so will your children, when they sin, be trodden upon by the nations of the world."

QUESTIONS

1) Why did Esau want to kill Jacob?
2) What did Rebecca say to Jacob?
3) What did Jacob see in his dream?
4) What was the promise God made to Jacob?
5) What did Jacob say when he awoke, and what did he call the name of the place?
6) Whom did Jacob meet at the well, and what did he ask them?
7) Who was Rachel?

XVII

JACOB IN LABAN'S HOUSE

Jacob stayed in the house of his uncle Laban for a month and tended his flock faithfully. Then Laban said to his nephew: "Because you are my sisters's son, should you work for me for nought? Tell me, what shall your wages be?"

Now Laban had two daughters: the name of the elder was Leah and the name of the younger was Rachel. Leah was afflicted with weak eyes, but Rachel was very beautiful. Jacob had fallen in love with Rachel, and he said to his uncle: "I will serve you seven years, if you will give me your younger daughter Rachel to wife."

Laban agreed, and Jacob served his uncle for seven years, tending his flocks day and night. His love for Rachel was so deep that the seven years of diligent work seemed to him but a few days. But in the end Laban deceived Jacob, and gave him to wife Leah instead of Rachel. When the seven years were over, Laban veiled the bride very heavily, as was the custom in the East, and no one could tell who she was. When the marriage was

over, Jacob realized that he had been deceived
by Laban and that he was given Leah instead of
Rachel. Jacob complained to his uncle: "Why
did you deceive me? Did I not serve you for
Rachel?"

"It is not the custom in our place for the younger
sister to be married before the elder," replied the

Jacob Tended Laban's Flock

cunning Laban; "serve me another term of seven
years and then I will give you Rachel also."

Jacob served Laban seven years longer and
married Rachel too. Laban gave Leah his servant
Zilpah as a handmaiden, and to Rachel he gave

as a handmaiden his servant Bilhah. Leah bore to Jacob six sons, whose names were: Reuben, Simeon, Levi, Judah, Issacher and Zebulun, and one daughter, Dinah. Rachel at first had no children, and she was very unhappy. After many years, she at last bore a son to Jacob who was named Joseph.

In accordance with the custom in the East, Jacob also married the handmaidens of his two wives, and each bore two sons. Bilhah's sons were named Dan and Naphtali, and Zilpah's sons were called Gad and Asher.

At the end of the fourteen years, Jacob asked his uncle's leave to go back to his own country Canaan. But Laban was unwilling to part with his son-in-law, because he was an excellent breeder of cattle, and under his care Laban's flocks had multiplied immensely. Laban begged Jacob to remain with him, promising him cattle in payment of his services. Jacob agreed to that and he stayed six more years with Laban. During these years, Jacob became the possessor of a great number of goats, sheep and camels, as well as many male and female slaves.

Even at the end of the twenty years, Laban was unwilling to let Jacob go. So one day, Jacob took his family and all his property and secretly started for his father's home in Canaan. Rachel took along her father's idols. Laban was, at that time, a distance away from his home to shear his sheep. On the third day, Laban was told that Jacob had fled, and he immediately got together his men and pursued Jacob.

Jacob and his men had already crossed the river, when Leban and his men overtook them on the seventh day. That night God appeared to Laban in a dream, and said to him: "Take heed that you speak not to Jacob either good or bad." On the following morning, Laban met Jacob, and said to him: "Why have you gotten away secretly from me, and carried away my daughters as though they were captives of the sword? Now, I have the power to do you harm, but I was warned by the God of your fathers not to you harm. But why have you stolen my gods?"

"I left secretly," replied Jacob, "because I was afraid that you would take away your daughters from me by force. As for your gods, with whomsoever you find them shall not live." Jacob did not know that Rachel had stolen them.

Laban searched all the tents for his gods, but they were nowhere to be found. Rachel put the idols in the saddle of her camel, and sat upon them. Jacob, angered by Laban's groundless accusation, said: "Why did you so hotly pursue after me? Have I taken anything of yours with me? For twenty years I have served you faithfully; in the daytime the heat consumed me, and the frost by night. If any injury came to your cattle, I bore the loss. I worked even fourteen years for my wives, and now you intend to do me harm when I long to return to my father's house with my honest-ly-gotten possessions."

"After all," replied Laban, "what you have, you earned in my house. Come! Let us make peace."

So they piled up a heap of stones on the far side of the Jordan, as a border between their lands, and they swore henceforth not to molest one another in any way. Laban returned to Mesopo-tamia, and Jacob continued on his way towards Canaan.

AGADAH

Leah Weeps Over Her Fate

The neighbors would tell Leah, the eldest daughter of Laban, that her aunt Rebecca gave birth to two sons, the elder of which was named Esau, and the younger Jacob. The elder son was very wicked, while the younger was good and righteous. She was then told by her neighbors that she, being the elder daughter of Laban, would have to get married to Esau, and her younger sister Rachel would be married to Jacob. For many days, even years, Leah prayed to God and continually wept that he spare her the great misfortune of becoming the wife of the wicked Esau. Thus she wept over her fate until her eyelashes dropped from her lids; and her prayers were heard in heaven.

QUESTIONS

1) For whom did Jacob agree to serve seven years, and how did he happen to get Leah instead?
2) What excuse did Laban offer to Jacob?
3) How many sons were born to Jacob in the house of Laban, and by whom?
4) How many years did Jacob stay in the house of Laban?
5) Tell how Jacob left Laban's house.
6) Why did Laban abstain from doing harm to Jacob?
7) Give an account of what took place after that.

XVIII
JACOB IN CANAAN

On his journey homeward, Jacob recollected that he would have to meet his brother Esau from whom he had fled so many years ago. In his desire to become reconciled with his brother, he sent messengers ahead to beg Esau to make peace with him. But the messengers soon returned with the news that Esau was already on his way from mount Seir, the place where he lived, with four hundred men.

This news struck terror into the heart of Jacob, and he began devising plans how to appease the anger of his brother. He prepared a handsome present for his brother, consisting of sheep, camels and other kinds of cattle which he sent ahead with some of his slaves. He also prayed to God for assistance: "O God of my father Abraham, and God of my father Isaac! I am not worthy of all the mercies which you have shown to me, your servant. When I first crossed this Jordan, I had nothing with me save my staff, and now I have such a large camp with me. Deliver me,

I pray you, from the hand of my brother Esau; for I fear him, lest he come and smite me, and the mother with the children."

Jacob then divided all his men and flocks into two groups, for he said: "If Esau comes and smites one group, then the other group will be able to escape."

As Esau drew near, Jacob went forward and bowed seven times to the ground before him. Esau, touched by his brother's humility, embraced and kissed him. Both of them wept, all their former enmity forgotten. Jacob then offered his gift to his brother who at first refused to accept it, but Jacob begged him so hard that he finally consented to take it. The two brothers then separated again, Esau returned to Seir, where he afterwards became the father of the warlike tribes of Edom who settled in the south of Canaan, and Jacob continued his journey towards Hebron.

When Jacob reached Bethel, God appeared to him, and said: "Your name shall henceforth not be Jacob but Israel (which means: Champion of the Lord)." God then blessed him and said: "You shall be the father of many tribes, and many kings shall descend from you. The land which I gave to Abraham and to Isaac to you will I give it and to your children."

On the road leading to Bethlehem, a second son was born to Rachel, but she died at the child's birth. The child was named Benjamin by his father. Jacob buried his beloved wife on the road to Bethlehem, and set up a monument upon her grave which can still be seen there. Now the sons of Jacob numbered twelve in all. These sons were the fathers of the twelve tribes, who afterwards formed the Jewish nation.

Finally Jacob made his way to Hebron, where his father Isaac lived, and there stayed near his father. Not very long after, Isaac died at the age of one hundred and eighty years. Esau and Jacob buried their father in the Cave of Machpelah, the family vault of Abraham, where previously Rebecca had also been buried.

After the death of Isaac, Jacob became the chief of the Hebrews.

AGADAH

Jacob Wrestles with an Angel.

When Jacob sent ahead a gift to his brother Esau, he and his wives and children remained over night in the camp. At midnight Jacob arose and first took his wives and his children across the brook of Jabbok, and then he took across his herds and his tents. On the other side of the brook, Jacob bethought himself of a few jars which he had left on the other side, and he went to fetch them. As Jacob was putting the jars in order, he noticed a human form standing near him.

"Who are you?" inquired Jacob.

"I am a shepherd," said he; "I worked very hard to-day and now I am tired. Look at that big herd of sheep behind me. I must take them all across the brook, and I am weary. Pray take these sheep across the brook for me and I will carry your jars."

Jacob agreed and began to carry the lambs across the brook. But to his great surprise the more sheep he carried across the more there remained behind. At last he lost patience. He fell upon the shepherd and caught him by the throat crying out: "Are you a magician? Is this a magic flock of cattle?"

"Do you wish to know what I am?" replied the stranger. "I will show you." Thereupon he touched the ground with the little finger, and flames burst forth, which consumed all the sheep. Jacob was not daunted by these wonderful feats. The shepherd then assumed the form of an angel, and wrestled with him till daybreak. The angel, angered because he did not come out victorious in the strife, touched the thigh of Jacob. This touch put the thigh out of joint and caused Jacob to limp.

As dawn drew night, the angel said: "Pray, Jacob, let me go, because it is near dawn."

"Are you a thief that you are afraid of the dawn of day?" asked Jacob.

"At daybreak all angels assemble before the Almighty to sing his praise," said the angel; "pray let me fly to heaven."

"I will not let you go," said Jacob, "and the angels will sing the praises of God without you."

"Should I fail to appear once, I shall not be allowed to participate in the singing any more," pleaded the angel.

But Jacob said: "I will not let you go, except you bless me."

At this moment, many troups of angels came down from heaven and said to the angel detained by Jacob: "The time to sing praises has come; make haste and fly with us to heaven, lest the time for singing pass."

Jacob refused to give him permission, and at last the angel blessed Jacob and said to him: "Your name shall be changed to Israel, for you have wrestled with an angel of God, and you have come out victorious.

QUESTIONS

1) What did Jacob do to become reconciled with his brother, and what did the messengers inform him?
2) What did Jacob do when he obtained this information?
3) Describe what occurred when the two brothers met.
4) What did God say to Jacob when he reached Beth-el?
5) Tell what happened to Rachel.
6) How many sons did Jacob have now, and what were their names?
7) How old was Isaac when he died, and who became the chief of the Hebrews after his death?

XIX
JOSEPH IS SOLD INTO SLAVERY

Jacob finally settled in the land of Canaan, where he and his sons were shepherds. Because Joseph was the son of his much-beloved Rachel, Jacob loved him more than the rest of his sons. To show that Joseph was his favorite he made him a princely garment, a coat of many colors, and this excited the envy of Joseph's brothers. In addition, Joseph would fan the jealousy and hatred of his brothers by careless words and actions.

One day Joseph came to his brothers and said: "I dreamt that we were all together in the field, binding sheaves. Then my sheaf stood up, and your sheaves surrounded mine and bowed to it."

His brothers flew into a rage and said: "Shall you indeed reign over us? Or shall you indeed have dominion over us?"

Another time Joseph told his father and his brothers of another dream. He said: "I dreamt that the sun, the moon and eleven stars bowed down to me."

Jacob rebuked Joseph for this dream, and he said: "What is the meaning of this dream that you dreamt? Shall I, your mother and your brothers indeed come to bow to you?"

His brothers hated him all the more because of that.

One day, the brothers took their flocks to Shechem, and Jacob said to Joseph, who was then seventeen years old: "Go and see whether all is well with your brothers and their flocks."

Joseph knew that his brothers hated him and that they might do him harm, yet he obeyed his father and went to look for his brothers in Shechem. When Joseph at last arrived there, and his brothers caught sight of him, they said to one another: "Here comes the dreamer! Come! let us kill him, and cast him into one of the pits, and we shall tell our father that an evil beast has devoured him."

"Let our hands shed no blood," said Reuben, the eldest, to his brothers. "Let us cast him into one of the pits in the wilderness and leave him there to die."

When Joseph reached them, his brothers stripped him of his many colored coat, threw him into a pit in the field and sat down to eat. While eating they saw a caravan of Ishmaelite traders coming, their camels laden with spices and drugs.

Seeing them, Judah said to his brothers: "What profit will there be in taking the life of our

Jacob Recognized Joseph's Coat

brother? Let us rather sell him to the Ishmaelites as a slave."

So the brothers took Joseph out of the pit and sold him to the Ishmaelites for twenty pieces of silver. The sale was made in the absence of Reuben, and when he returned and did not find Joseph in the pit, he cried out in despair: "The lad is not there! Where shall I go now?"

Then the brothers took the coat of Joseph and dipped it into the blood of a kid. They brought the bloody coat to their aged father and said: "This coat we found in the wilderness; see whether it is not Joseph's coat."

Jacob recognized the coat, and he cried out: "Alas, this is my son's coat! Some wild beast has torn him to pieces and devoured him!"

The unhappy father rent his clothes, and mourned for his beloved son many days. Every member of the family tried to console Jacob, but he would not be comforted, saying: "Nay, but I will go down to the grave mourning."

AGADAH

On the Tomb of His Mother

Joseph went along with the Ishmaelites until they reached his mother's tomb in the evening. It was moonlight, and the caravan rested. Grief overcame Joseph. He fell upon the grave, burst forth into bitter tears and cried: "O mother, mother! I am an outcast and a slave, I, the child of the wife Jacob loved best. When you were dying, you bade my father look at me and be comforted for his loss. O mother, mother! have you no thought for your son? Awake and see the sad plight of your child; shake off your sleep; be my defense against my brothers, and comfort my father. Awake and look upon the desolation of the soul of my father who cherished you, and who for fourteen years served in bondage for you, his beloved Rachel! Console him, I pray you, and by the voice that he loved soothe the grief of his last days."

A low voice issued from the tomb: "My son! my son Joseph, my child! I have heard your cries. I know all you have suffered, and my grief is as deep as the sea. But put your trust in God. Rise my child, and have patience. If you knew the future you would be comforted."

———

QUESTIONS

1) Why did the brothers hate Joseph?
2) What were the two dreams that Joseph dreamt?
3) What did the brothers say when they saw Joseph come?
4) Who disuaded them from doing it?
5) Tell how they happened to sell Joseph.
6) What did they do after they sold Joseph?
7) What did Jacob say when he was shown the bloody coat?

XX
JOSEPH IS CAST IN PRISON

The Ishmaelites brought Joseph to Egypt, and there sold him as a slave to Potiphar, chief of the king's bodyguard. Joseph was loyal to his master, and therefore he did not remain a common slave for a long time. Potiphar soon promoted Joseph to be the steward of his household.

Joseph proved to be a skilfull manager, and everything prospered in his hands. But Joseph was unfortunate in that he gained the high esteem and love not only of his master Potiphar, but also that of his master's wife. The young, handsome Joseph pleased her so much that she began to make love to him and pleaded with him to elope with her. The noble-hearted Joseph refused to deceive his kind master, and he therefore spurned her love. Daily she urged him to betray Potiphar, but he sternly refused.

Infuriated at Joseph's fidelity, she one day took hold of his coat. Joseph, unwilling to listen to her, fled out of the house, but his coat, by which she had been holding him, remained in her hands.

She then began to scream to her servants for help. When Potiphar came home, she complained to him that her Hebrew slave had tried to attack her. Potiphar believed his wife's story, and had Joseph thrown into prison for his crime.

Joseph remained in prison for a long time. But even there he won the admiration of all those who came in contact with him, and the warden of the prison made Joseph supervisor over all the other prisoners. Among the prisoners that were put under Joseph's care were two officers of the king's court, one the king's chief butler and the other his chief baker. They were imprisoned there by the order of Pharaoh, king of Egypt, for negligence in performing their duties.

One morning, while Joseph was making his rounds in prison, he noticed that the king's officers were extremely sad. When he asked them for the cause of their grief, they replied that both of them happened to have had strange dreams during the night and that there was no one in prison to interpret it for them.

"Do not interpretations belong to God?" replied Joseph; "Tell it to me, I pray you."

The king's officers accepted Joseph's offer. First the chief-butler related his dream to Joseph, which ran as follows:

"In my dream I saw a vine before me; and in the vine were three branches; and as it was budding, its blossoms opened, and the clusters produced ripe grapes. Pharaoh's cup was in my hand. I took the grapes, pressed them into Pharaoh's cup, and handed the cup to him."

"This is the interpretation," said Joseph. "The three branches are three days. Within three days Pharaoh shall release you from prison and restore you to your office; you will hand Pharaoh his cup, as you used to do when you were his cup-bearer."

"But pray," pleaded Joseph with the cup bearer, "say a kind word for me to the king when you get out; for indeed I was stolen away out of the land of the Hebrews, and here also I have done nothing that they should put me in prison."

When the baker saw that the interpretation was favorable, he too related his dream to Joseph: "In my dream I saw three baskets of white bread on my head; in the upper basket there were all sorts of pastry for Pharaoh, but the birds kept on eating them out of the basket on my head."

"This is the interpretation of your dream," said Joseph in a very sad voice: "Within three days Pharaoh shall hang you on a tree; and the birds shall eat your flesh off you."

Joseph's interpretations came true: the chief baker was hanged, and the chief butler was set free and returned to his former office at the king's court. But the chief butler forgot all about Joseph, and made no mention of him to the king.

AGADAH

Joseph Is Punished

When Joseph said to the chief butler: "Pray, say a kind word to the king when you are free, and take me out too," a heavenly voice was heard saying: "Because you have left your trust in me, and you have instead reposed in man, the chief butler shall not think of you when he is out of prison, and you shall remain imprisoned until it is my desire that you be set free."

QUESTIONS

1) Whose slave did Joseph become when in Egypt?
2) Why was Joseph put in prison?
3) Who was with Joseph in prison?
4) What did the chief-butler dream, and what was the interpretation Joseph gave him?
5) What did Joseph request of the chief-butler?
6) What did the chief-baker dream, and how did Joseph interpret it.

XXI
FROM A PRISON TO A THRONE

Two years later, the king of Egypt himself had a very strange dream. It seemed to him that he stood on the brink of the River Nile, and out of the river came up seven fat cows that broused over a meadow. Then seven very lean cows came up out of the river and devoured the fat ones. He further dreamt that seven full ears of corn grew on one stalk. Then seven thin ears grew up, and the lean ears devoured the full ones.

When Pharaoh awoke, he was very much troubled by his dreams, and he summoned to his court all his priests and his magicians to explain the dreams to him, but no one could interpret them. The king's butler then thought of Joseph, and he told the king all about his dream and also that of the chief baker.

So by the command of Paraoh Joseph was immediately taken out of prison and brought before him. The king said to Joseph: "They tell me that you can interpret dreams."

"It is not in me," answered Joseph modestly,

"but perhaps God may explain it to you, O king, through me."

Joseph Before Pharaoh

So Pharaoh related his dreams to Joseph, who thereupon said: "The two dreams mean one and the same thing: The seven fat cows and the seven full ears of grain mean that there will be seven years of plenty in the land of Egypt. There will be a great abundance of grain during these seven years. The seven lean cows and the seven thin ears of grain mean that after this period of plenty there will arise seven years of famine. The crops during those seven years will be very poor, and there will be great famine in the land of Egypt. Therefore I would advise the king to seek out a wise man, and let him lay up vast stores of grain during the seven years of plenty, so that when the seven years of famine come, the people may be supplied with food out of those stores, and not starve.

Pharaoh was delighted with Joseph's interpretation of the dreams and with his advice, and he said to his courtiers: "Can we find a man like this in whom is the spirit of God?"

Turning to Joseph, the king said: "Since God has shown you all this, there is no better man to be set over the land than you yourself. By you shall my people be ruled; only in the throne shall I be greater than you."

Pharaoh then gave Joseph his signet ring, put a gold chain about his neck and made him ride in his own chariot throughout the city. When the new official drove through the streets, everybody bowed low before him.

So, at the age of thirty, Joseph became viceroy of

the land of Egypt. Joseph married Esnath, the daughter of an Egyptian priest, and she bore him two sons. He called the elder Manasseh, and the younger he called Ephraim.

The seven years of plenty came, as Joseph had prophesied. During those years of plenty, Joseph stored away immense quantities of grain, and later on, when the seven years of famine arose he sold the grain to the hungry people. There was so much grain in the land of Egypt in the years of famine that even people from other countries came to Egypt to buy corn.

AGADAH

The Magicians Try to Interpret the Dream.

Early in the morning Pharaoh summoned all the magicians and all the wise men of the land to appear before him and interpret his dreams. Some of the magicians said: "The seven fat cows show that you will beget seven daughters, and the seven lean cows swallowing the seven fat cows signify that your seven daughters will die. As for the seven ears of corn, they tend to show that you will conquer seven lands, and seven other lands will rebel against you."

"This explanation pleases me not," shouted the king in great fury. "Away with you."

Another group of magicians and wise men offered the following explanation: "The seven tribes of Canaan will wage war against seven fortified cities of Egypt and conquer them; then the seven conquered cities will rebel against them and defeat them. As for the dream of the seven ears of corn, it means that the king will marry seven wives all of whom will die during his lifetime. Then the fourteen sons of the king will fight with one another, and the seven young ones will prevail over the seven older ones."

"Why all this folly!" exclaimed the king in disappointment. "Begone, or you shall all suffer the penalty of death."

Thereupon the chief butler told Pharaoh about Joseph. He laid stress upon the fact that Joseph was a slave and a Hebrew so as to show that he does not deserve to be promoted to a high office.

QUESTIONS

1) What did Pharaoh dream?
2) How did Joseph interpret the dreams?
3) What was the advice Joseph gave to Pharaoh?
4) What did Pharaoh say then?
5) What were the names of Joseph's two sons?
6) Was the famine confined only to the land of Egypt?

XXII

JOSEPH'S BROTHERS IN EGYPT

Canaan also suffered from the great famine, and when Jacob learned that food could be bought in Egypt, he sent his sons there to buy food. Ten of them set out for Egypt; Benjamin, the youngest, being left behind with his father.

Joseph supervised the sale of the grain personally, for he knew that his brothers would some day come to Egypt to buy food. When the sons of Jacob came into the presence of Joseph, he at once recognized them, but they did not recognize him. He pretended to speak roughly to them through an interpreter, and accused them of being spies. The brothers, in defense, said: "We are no spies. We are twelve sons of one father; one of our brothers was lost, and the youngest one is staying behind with our father in Canaan. We have come into Egypt not to spy out the land, but to buy grain."

Joseph pretended not to believe them, and he said: "It is not true; you are spies, and you have come to make observations of the land. If you are indeed honest men, I will keep you all in prison, and let one of you return to Canaan and fetch your younger brother here."

The brothers looked at one another, and said: "We are verily guilty concerning our brother. We saw him suffer, we heard his entreaties, yet we had no pity for him. Now we are punished for the wrong."

Joseph heard all they said, for they did not suppose for a moment that the haughty Egpytian ruler understood their language, since he spoke to them through an interpreter. Their words moved Joseph so deeply that he had to turn aside to hide his tears.

Joseph kept all his brothers in prison for three days, and then he said to them: "You may all return to Canaan to your father to carry food to your families, but you must leave one brother as hostage here. But do not dare come here again, without bringing your youngest brother with you."

Joseph commanded that their bags be filled with grain, and that the money which they had brought to buy grain be put back into their bags. He then detained one of their brothers, Simeon, as hostage, and let the rest go home.

As they came to an inn to put up for the night, one of the brothers opened his sack to get fodder for his donkey and found his money at the mouth of the sack.   Bewildered, he shouted out to his brothers: "My money is restored; and, lo, it is even in my sack." The brothers tremblingly turned to each other saying: "What is this that God has done to us?"

The brothers returned to Canaan and told their father all that had happend.   The brothers then emptied their bags of corn, and each and every one of them found in his sack the money he had given to Joseph's steward for the corn.   The brothers trembled with fear, and the broken hearted Jacob said bitterly: "Me have you bereaved of my children: Joseph is not and Simeon is not, and now you will take Benjamin away.   My son shall not go with you; if harm befall him on the way, then you will bring down my gray hairs with sorrow to the grave."

AGADAH

The Brothers Are Repentant

When one of the brothers found the money in his bag in the inn, the brothers trembled greatly at the sight of the money, and some of them said: "Where then is the loving-kindness of God toward our fathers Abraham, Isaac and Jacob? Yea, he has delivered us into the hands of the Egyptian ruler that he may raise accusations against us and punish us."

Judah said to the complaining brothers: "Indeed, we are guilty concerning our brother Joseph. We have sinned against God in that we sold our brother, our flesh and blood, into slavery. Why then do you complain saying: 'Where is the loving-kindness of God towards our fathers?'"

"Did I not say to you: 'Do not sin against the lad?'" asked Reuben. "But you would not listen to me. Now the Lord does demand him from our hands. How then can we complain and say: 'Where is the loving-kindness of God towards our fathers?'"

QUESTIONS

1) How many brothers went to Egypt to buy corn? Who remained in Canaan?
2) What did Joseph say to his brothers when he recognized them?
4) Why did Joseph weep?
5) What happened in the inn?
6) What did Jacob say when he heard his sons' story?

XXIII
JOSEPH REVEALS HIS IDENTITY

The famine in the land of Canaan continued, and the grain which the sons of Jacob had brought from Egypt finally was exhausted. Jacob again asked his sons to go to Egypt and buy food, but his sons replied: "The ruler of the land of Egypt expressly told us not to come there without our youngest brother. How then can we go now without Benjamin?"

Reuben tried to persude his father to let Benjamin go, but in vain, Jacob would not let him go. Then Judah, the leader among his brothers, came forward and said: "Send the lad with us and we will go, so that we may live and not die from starvation, both we and you, and our little ones. I will be surety for him; if I bring him not back to you, then let me bear the blame for ever."

The words of Judah won Jacob over. He blessed his sons, and prayed to God to protect them from evil in the foreign land. He also sent a little present of honey, spices, nuts and almonds to the Egyptian ruler, and he told his sons to return the money which had been placed in their bags.

When the brothers appeared before Joseph the second time, he asked: "Is your old father of whom you spoke well?"

They bowed before the Egyptian ruler, and replied: "He is well."

At the sight of Benjamin, Joseph was so overcome that he went into his private chamber and wept. He washed his face, and when he came out again, he invited his brothers to dine with him. Much to their surprise, the brothers were served according to their age.

After they had purchased fresh supplies in Egpyt and were about to return home, Joseph ordered again that the money, which they had brought with which to buy grain, be put secretly in their sacks, and that his silver cup be put in Benjamin's sack. The brothers had not gone very far, when they were overtaken by an Egyptian official who had been sent by Joseph. The official spoke harshly to the brothers from Canaan, saying: "Why have you rewarded evil for good? You stole the silver cup of my lord!"

The brothers felt indignant at this accusation and replied: "We are honest men; we did not steal your lord's cup. With whomever you will find the cup let him die, and we also will be slaves of your master."

The brothers immediately opened their sacks, and to their great horror the cup was found in Benjamin's sack. In their grief they rent their clothes. They returned to the city and there they were brought once more into the presence of the haughty ruler of Egypt. They bowed to Joseph again, and said: "What can we say to our lord in our defense? How can we justify ourselves? We will all be your slaves."

"O no," said Joseph, "that would not be just. The one in whose sack the cup was found shall be my slave, and the rest of you may go up in peace to your father."

Judah, who was surety to his aged father that he would bring Benjamin back in safety, now came forward and pleaded with Joseph: "My lord, permit me to say a few words to you. When we came to Egypt to buy food, you asked if we had a father or a brother. We told you that we had an old father, and a younger brother; that the brother of this our youngest brother was dead, and he was the only one left of his mother; and that his father loved him dearly. Then you took us for spies, and you commanded us to bring our youngest brother with us when we come again to buy grain. We told you that the lad could not leave his father, lest his father die. But my lord insisted and said that we could not see you again unless we brought our

younger brother with us. Our old father refused
to let him go, saying: 'If any harm befall him,
you will bring down my gray hairs with sorrow
to the grave.' If then we now return without
the lad, our aged father will be unable to bear
it, and we shall have caused his untimely death.
I was surety for the lad to my father, and told him
that if I fail to bring the lad back, then I shall

"I am your brother Joseph"

bear the blame for ever. Therefore, pray, let me
stay as a bondman instead of the young lad, and
permit him to go back to his father with his
brothers."

This simple forward story of Judah so touched
the heart of Joseph that he was unable to restrain
himself any longer. He orderd all the Egyptians

out of the room, and he burst into tears, and said: "I am your brother Joseph whom you sold into Egypt as a slave."

The brothers were too alarmed to answer, but Joseph quieted them with the words: "Do not grieve over the fact that you sold me, for God himself sent me here in order that I might preserve your lives. He made me Pharaoh's chief adviser and ruler of all Egypt. Now, return hastily to our father and tell him of all my greatness in this land. Bring him here with all his possessions, so that you may all live with me in this country from now on."

Joseph then embraced his brothers and kissed them, and they all shed tears of joy. Pharaoh and his servants were well pleased upon the report that Joseph's brothers had come to Egypt. The king of Egypt provided the brothers with beasts of burden and wagons in which they were to bring their father with all his possessions. To Joseph the king said: "Invite your father and all his household to come here, and I will give them the good of the land of Egypt.

AGADAH

Judah's Courage

Upon Joseph's refusal to let Benjamin return to his father, Judah, the great hero, became exceedingly wroth, and he said to Joseph: "Return Benjamin to us or I shall dye the whole land of Egypt with blood."

"Oh, yes, you and your brothers are famous dyers," replied Joseph; "you dyed the city of Shechem with blood, and also the coat of your lost brother you dyed with blood and brought it to your father saying: 'An evil beast has devoured him.'"

Judah then began to plead with Joseph. But the ruler of Egypt remained unmoved and he said to Judah: "Why do you speak so much, while your older brothers stand by silent?"

"I alone was surety to my father for my brother Benjamin, saying: 'If I do not bring him back to you, let me bear the blame forever, in this world and in the world to come,'" replied Judah.

"Why did you not stand by your other brother when he was sold for twenty pieces of silver? You then disregarded the great grief of your father and said: 'This coat have we found.' Your lost brother had done no evil, while this Benjamin is a thief. Go then to your aged father and tell him that his son too was devoured by a beast."

The rage of Judah knew no bounds, and turning to Naphtali, who was very swift of leg said: "Go forth and count all the streets of the city."

The swift messenger soon returned and reported that there were twelve streets in the city. "Now, brothers," thereupon Judah said, "behave yourselves like men, and let us destroy the whole city to save our brother. I will take upon myself to destroy three streets, and each and every one of you one street, and thus we will destroy Egypt as we destroyed Shechem."

When Pharaoh learned of what was going on in the house of Joseph, he advised Joseph to grant the Hebrews their request.

QUESTIONS

1) What made Jacob at last yield in sending Benjamin to Egypt?
2) Tell what happened when Joseph saw Benjamin.
3) What did Joseph order when his brothers were about to leave Egypt?
4) What did the brothers say when they were accused of stealing the cup?
5) Why did Judah offer to remain a slave instead of Benjamin?
6) Describe what took place then.
7) What did Pharaoh say when he heard about Joseph's brothers?

XXIV
DEATH OF JACOB AND JOSEPH

With joyous hearts the brothers now returned to Canaan, and as soon as they entered the house of their aged father, they said: "Glad tidings! Joseph is still alive, and he is the ruler of Egypt."

Jacob did not believe them, for it was indeed too good to be true. But when he saw the royal wagons and the beasts that had been sent by Joseph, he exclaimed: "It is enough; Joseph my son is yet alive; I will go down and see him before I die."

Soon afterwards, Jacob left for Egypt with his entire household, numbering in all seventy souls. Judah acted as herald in informing Joseph of their father's arrival at the borders of Egypt. Joseph made ready his royal chariot, and went out to meet his aged father. Father and son embraced and wept for a long time. Joseph then presented some of his brothers and his aged father before the King of Egypt, who was well pleased with their arrival.

At the desire of Joseph and with the consent of Pharaoh, Jacob and his family settled in Goshen the most fertile part of Egypt. The Hebrew settlers followed their occupation of cattle-breeding, and they lived apart from the Egyptians from whom they differed both in language and in customs.

Jacob was one hundred and thirty years old when he first came to Egypt, and there he lived for seventeen years. When he felt that his end was drawing nigh, he blessed all his sons. He also blessed the two sons of Joseph, Ephraim and Manasseh, and he expressed it as his wish that the two sons of Joseph be in after years considered the heads of two separate and distinct tribes.

Before his death, Jacob called for his sons, and blessed them, then he charged thus: "I am soon to die; pray do not bury me in the land of Egypt; bury me with my fathers in the Cave of Machpelah, in the land of Canaan. There they buried Abraham and Sarah his wife; there they buried Isaac and Rebecca his wife, and there I buried Leah."

Jacob died soon after, and his sons, with the consent of Pharaoh, took his body to Canaan, and there buried him in the Cave of Machpelah. For an escort the king sent all the chief men of his palace, and all the great men of Egypt together with many chariots and horsemen.

Coming back to Egypt after the funeral, the

brothers said: "Now that our father is dead, Joseph will repay us the evil we have done to him." They therefore sent a message to him: "Your father did command before he died, saying: 'Forgive, I pray you, the sin of your brothers in that they did evil to you.' And now we pray you to forgive the sin of the servants of your father."

Upon hearing this message, Joseph broke down in tears, and when his brothers came and bowed to him, he said to them: "Fear not; for am I in the place of God? And as for you, you meant evil against me; but God meant it for good."

When Joseph felt that he was about to die, he said to his brothers: "God will surely remember you, and bring you up to the land which he swore to Abraham, Isaac and Jacob, then you shall carry up my bones with you to the promised land."

Joseph died, being one hundred and ten years old. His body was embalmed, according to the Egyptian custom, and put in a coffin in Egypt.

AGADAH

How Jacob Received the News

When the brothers reached the boundary of Canaan, they said to one another: "How can we inform our father that Joseph is still alive? Such glad news may frighten him, and besides he may not believe us."

On drawing near to their homes, they beheld Serah the daughter of Asher, coming out to meet them. Serah was a very wise and beautiful maiden and was skilled in playing the harp. The brothers now thought of a good plan. They gave Serah a harp, and said to her: "Go and play before your grandfather Jacob, and sing the following words: 'Joseph, my uncle, lives! He is not dead. He is the ruler over the whole land of Egypt.'"

Serah took the harp and hurried towards Jacob's tent. On entering, she said: "Peace be with you dear grandfather."

"May peace be with you forever," came the reply.

She then sat down in front of Jacob, and with a very sweet melodious voice she sang the following words, accompanying herself upon the harp: "Joseph, my uncle, lives! Joseph, my uncle, lives! He is not dead! He is the ruler over the whole land of Egypt." She repeated these words several times, and her sweet music brought cheer and comfort to Jacob's sad heart.

"Continue singing these very delighful words, my child," said Jacob to Serah. She repeated the

song again and again, and Jacob grew more and
more cheerful. He then approached Serah, and
putting his hands on her head, said: "May death
never have power over you, for you have revived
my spirit." And so it was. Serah did not die, she
entered Paradise alive.

QUESTIONS

1) How was Jacob convinced at last that Joseph was
    alive?
2) What did Jacob say then?
3) Where did Jacob and his family settle?
4) How many years did Jacob dwell in Egypt, and how
    old was he when he died?
5) What was Jacob's wish with reference to the sons of
    Joseph, Ephraim and Manasseh?
6) How old was Joseph when he died, and what was his
    last wish?

XXV
THE EGYPTIAN BONDAGE

Abraham had other descendants besides Isaac, and Isaac likewise had other descendants besides Jacob. From these descendants there sprang forth many kindred Hebrew tribes. Now when the children or the tribes of the patriarch Jacob, whose name was changed to Israel, increased in number, they styled themselves "Sons of Israel" or "Israelites." This was to distinguish themselves from the other kindred Hebrew tribes.

Now the Israelites lived in Goshen, a province in northern Egypt, which is irrigated by a tributary of the Nile. There they formed almost a separate nation, living the life of simple shepherds, observing the customs, and speaking the language they had brought with them from Canaan. They remembered the teachings of their ancestors, and believed in one Supreme Being, the Creator of heaven and earth.

As the Israelites multiplied with great rapidity, the one tribe of Israel which consisted only of seventy souls when Jacob first came to Egypt now branched off into smaller tribes, who called themselves by the names of the sons of Jacob. Joseph's descendants branched off into two separate tribes, one the descendants of Ephraim, and the other the descendants of Manasseh. There were consequently thirteen tribes: Reuben, Simeon, Levi, Judah, Issacar, Zebulun, Dan, Naphtali, Gad, Asher, Ephraim, Manasseh and Benjamin. Each tribe had its own elders and chieftains, and, although there was no supreme chief over all the tribes, they remained united by the ties of common religious beliefs, a common language and a common origin.

In the course of time, many years after the death of Joseph, a new king succeeded to the throne of Egypt. This king feared the Israelites for they were becoming a vast and mighty people. He one day said to his people: "Behold the children of Israel are too many and too mighty for us; come let us deal wisely with them, lest they multiply and in case of war with other nations they join our enemies."

The king and his officials therefore decided to check the growth of the Israelites and to crush their spirit by making slaves of them. They were forced to do hard labor for the benfit of the state, digging ditches, building store-cities, erecting giant obelisks and pyramids and royal palaces. The poor slaves were given no assistance in their work, for they were forced to make even their own bricks.

The Egyptains were greatly enraged when they noticed that, in spite of the harsh treatment and overwork, the Israelites continued to increase with great rapidity. Pharaoh ordered the Hebrew nurses to murder every little boy as soon as he is born. But the nurses feared God and would not execute the king's command. God rewarded the nurses for their kindness. Finally, Pharaoh issued an order to all Egyptians that every new-born male child be cast into the River Nile, and that only the girls be allowed to live.

Great was the grief of the enslaved fathers and mothers upon seeing their children put to death by drowning. But in spite of this, the Israelites did not forget their ancestors, Abraham, Isaac and Jacob. They hoped some day to be freed from bondage and restored to the land which God had promised to their ancestors.

AGADAH

The Kind Women

When the king of Egypt made many attempts to diminish the number of the Israelites, a voice from heaven was heard saying: "I promised their father Abraham that I would make his children as numerous as the stars in heaven, and you, O wicked king, contrive to prevent them from multiplying. We shall see whose word will stand, mine or yours."

While the men of Israel slept exhausted after their unspeakable toil, their faithful women labored to relieve and strenghten them. They hastened to the springs to bring pure water for their husbands to drink, and, by the grace of the All Merciful, it so happened that their pitchers were found each time to contain half water and half fish.

These devoted and diligent women dressed the fish, and prepared other good meats for their husbands. They brought the food to their husbands in the field, and encouraged them with their cheerful words. This loving attention of the women soothed the hearts of the men and gave them fresh energy.

QUESTIONS

1) Why were the Hebrews named Israelites?
2) Where did the Israelites live?
3) How many tribes were there, and what were their names?
4) Why did the king fear the Israelites?
5) How was the king of the Egyptians called, and what did he do to curb the growth of the Israelites?
6) What was the hope of the Israelites?

XXVI
A GREAT LEADER IS BORN

In those days, so trying for the Israelites, their future deliverer was born. In the tribe of Levi there lived a man named Amram together with his wife Jochebed, their son Aaron and their daughter Miriam. When the cruel king's order was issued that all the new-born children of the Israelites be drowned in the Nile, Jochebed gave birth to a son. Fearing that the Egyptians might find the baby boy and drown him, she hid him for three months. But the time came when she could hide him no longer; so she put the baby in a water tight basket, carried it down to the bank of the Nile, and hid it among the rushes. She told her daughter Miriam, a girl of about eight years old, to stand a short distance away, watch it and keep it from harm.

At that hour the king's daughter and her maidens came to the river to bathe. The princess noticed the basket, and curious to know what it contained, she ordered one of her maidens to open it. And there lay a little baby boy crying bitterly. The princess took pity on the child, and she decided to save it and bring it up as her own. She remarked

"And there lay a little baby boy crying"

to her maidens: "This must be one of the Hebrews' children."

Little Miriam, then approached and said to the princess: "May I go and call a Hebrew woman to nurse the child for you?"

"Oh, yes," consented the princess.

Little Miriam quickly ran home and brought her own mother to take care of the baby. Pharaoh's daughter said to the woman: "Take this baby and nurse it for me, and I will pay you for it."

Joyfully the mother took the baby in her arms, carried it home and cared for it. When the boy grew old enough he was returned to the princess who brought him up as her own son and gave him the name of Moses, which means "one taken out of the water." Moses was thus brought up in the palace where he received an excellent education as became a prince of the royal household. But he knew and learnt from his mother and father that he was a Hebrew and that his people were suffering greatly.

With bitterness and indignation Moses watched his brothers being oppressed and insulted by the Egyptian overseers and task-masters who were appointed by the king to see to it that his orders should be carried out. Now and then Moses would go out among them and watch them at their hard labor. He would grieve for them, and hoped that some day he might find a way to set them free.

One day, as Moses left the palace to visit his brothers, he saw an Israelite being severely beaten by an Egyptian task-master. He was so angry at the unjust sufferings of his race that he took the law in his own hand and slew the Egyptian task-master. Moses believed that no one had witnessed his act, and he buried the body in sand. On the following day when Moses went out again, he saw two Hebrews fighting, and he said to the aggressor: "Why do you smite your neighbor?" The aggressor replied: "Who made you the ruler and judge over us? Do you intend to kill me as you killed the Egyptian?"

Pharaoh soon learnt what Moses had done, and Moses, to save his life, fled from Egypt and went into the desert that stretched across the shores of the Red Sea, between Egypt and Canaan.

AGADAH

Gabriel Saves Moses

One day Pharaoh was dining in his palace, with the queen at his right hand, his daughter Bithia with the boy Moses on her lap at his left. The infant took the crown from off the head of the king and placed it on his own head.

The king and his nobles were terrified. They thought that this action betokened that evil would come to the king through the child that was before them. Then Balaam, the son of Beor, spoke to the king saying: "My lord and king! It signifies that this child will some day take the crown from your head and put it on his own, and will enslave or destroy your people. My advice therefore is, O king, that you slay this child before he grows up and becomes a menace to you and to your people."

"We will take other counsel," said Pharaoh, "before we decide the fate of this child."

The angel Gabriel, in the form of an old man, appeared with the councillors, and he said thus: "Let no innocent blood be shed. The child is too young to know what he is doing. Prove whether he has any understanding, before you sentence him to death. O king! let a bowl of live coals and a bowl of precious stones be placed before the little one. If he takes the stones, then he has understanding, but if he stretches his hand toward the burning coals, then we shall know that he is innocent and that he took the crown without any purpose or design."

The advice pleased the king, and he ordered his servants to do as the angel had suggested.

When the basins were brought in and offered to Moses, he thrust out his hands to reach the jewels. But Gabriel, who had made himself invisible, caught his hand and directed it towards the red-hot coals. The coals burnt the child's hand, and he lifted it and touched his mouth with it, thus burning part of his lips and part of his tongue; and this explains why Moses said, in after days: "I am slow of lips and slow of tongue."

Pharaoh and his councillors were now convinced of the simplicity of Moses, and no harm was done him.

QUESTIONS

1) Who was Jochebed, and who were her children?
2) What did Jochebed do when a new baby was born to her?
3) Who happened to come to the Nile then, and what happened?
4) Who was watching over the baby, and what did she say to the princess?
5) Whom did Miriam bring to take care of the baby?
6) Who named the baby *Moses*, and what does it mean?
7) Tell why Moses had to flee from Egypt?

XXVII
THE MISSION

Moses wandered through the desert until he came to a place where lived a tribe of nomad shepherds, the Midianites, kinsmen of the Hebrews. He sat down at a little distance from a well and watched seven maidens approach the well, fill the troughs with water for their sheep to drink. They were the daughters of the Midianite priest Jethro. They hardly finished filling the troughs, when shepherds came and drove them away from the well. Moses hastened to the aid of the maidens and helped them water their flock.

When the maidens came home with their flocks, they told their father that a stranger from Egypt had protected them from the rough shepherds and helped them water their flocks. And the priest said to his daughters: "Where is the stranger? Why did you not invite him to our house? Call him that he may eat bread with us."

Moses was pleased to remain in the house of the Midianite priest, and, in the course of time, he married one of his daughters, Zipporah. In Midian, Moses took up the occupation of his ancestors, and he kept the flocks of Jethro. Even while minding the sheep, Moses did not cease to brood over the sad plight of his brothers who were held in slavery by the Egyptians. He was forever devising plans by which they might become free men.

One day, while tending the sheep of his father-in-law, he advanced farther into the desert than usual, and there he saw before him a thorn-bush all ablaze, and though it burnt, the flames did not appear to consume it. He was about to come nearer, when he suddenly heard a voice speaking to him from the midst of the burning bush: "Moses, Moses, take off your shoes, for you are standing upon holy ground. I am the Lord God of your fathers, the God of Abraham, Isaac and Jacob. I have seen the sorrows of my people in Egypt; I have heard their cry by reason of their task-masters. I am come down to deliver them out of the hands of the Egyptians and to bring them into a large land, flowing with milk and honey. The cry of the children of Israel has come to me. Come now therefore, and I will send you to Pharaoh, that you may bring forth my people the children of Israel out of Egypt."

Moses answered with great awe and fear: "Who am I that I should go to Pharaoh and set the Israelites free? And if I go to the children of Israel and tell them that the God of our fathers sent me, they will ask: 'What is his name?' Then how shall I answer them?"

God replied: "I am he who is eternal. Tell the children of Israel that the Lord God of their fore-fathers, the God of Abraham, Isaac and Jacob, sent you to them. The children of Israel will hearken to you, and you together with the elders of Israel shall go to the king of Egypt and tell him that the Lord God of the Hebrews desires that he permit the Israelites go out of his land."

Moses said: "O Lord God, but the people will not believe me that you appeared to me."

God told Moses to perform three miracles before the people so that they might believe him. His rod will be changed into a serpent and then back into a rod; his hand will become leprous when put into his bossom, and water taken from the Nile will be changed into blood when spilt on the ground.

Moses again demurred: "Oh, Lord, I am not a man of words. I am slow of speech, and of slow tongue."

God replied again: "Who has made man's mouth? or who makes a man dumb, or deaf, or seeing or blind? Is it not I the Lord? Now Aaron your brother, will be your spokesman unto the people."

Finally, Moses resolved to accept God's mission. He returned to his father-in-law's house, and, taking his wife and his two sons with him, he set forth on his perilous task of freeing the Israelites from bondage.

On the way to Egypt, Moses met his brother Aaron, and upon the latter's advice, Moses sent back his wife and children to Midian. When the two messengers of God entered Egypt, they gathered together the elders of the tribes, and told them that the God of their forefathers had sent them to free the people from bondage. The Israelites believed the words of the two brothers, and they were overjoyed at the news. Moses and Aaron then went to the court of the Egyptian king, and told him that the God of the Hebrews desires that his people be permitted to go to the wilderness and there worship him.

The king listened scornfully, and he asked: "And who is this God that I should obey him?" I will not let the Israelites go. Leave them alone to do their work, and you look after your own affairs."

As a result of the first visit of Moses and Aaron, the king of Egypt ordered his task-masters to see that the Israelites worked harder than ever. Until that time the Hebrew builders have been supplied with straw which they mixed with clay in making their bricks. Now the king of Egypt ordered that the Hebrews must go and gather straw in the fields for themselves, and that at the same time they must make the same daily amount of bricks.

One day as Moses met some of his unfortunate brothers, he was rebuked by them: "You have made our lot worse than before; why do you not let us alone?"

Moses was very much discouraged at seeing the sad plight of his brothers, but he was soon encouraged by the word of God: "Now shall you see what I will do to Pharaoh; he shall let my people go by being shown a strong hand."

AGADAH

The Good Shepherd

Moses watched over Jethro's flock with loving care, and he took care that no harm befall the herds entrusted to him. He also took great care that his flock do no harm to other men's property. He always chose an open meadow as his pasturing place, to prevent his sheep from grazing in private fields.

One day while Moses was tending the flock in a barren place, he saw that one of the lambs had left the flock and was trying to escape. The good shepherd pursued it, but the lamb ran so much the faster, and fled through valley and over hill, till it reached a mountain stream; then it halted and drank.

Moses now came up to it, looked at it with troubled countenance and said: "My dear little friend! Then it was thirst that made you run so far and seem to flee from me; and I knew it not! Poor little creature, how tired you must be!"

Moses then took up the lamb, placed it upon his shoulders, and carried it back to the flock.

While Moses was carrying the lamb, there came a voice from heaven: "You, who have shown such great love, such great patience towards sheep, are surely worthy to be called upon to shepherd my people the children of Israel.

QUESTIONS

1) What happened to Moses at the well in Midiam, and whom did Moses marry?
2) What did Moses happen to see one day?
3) What did a voice say to him?
4) Did Moses want to go on the Mission, and what excuses did he offer?
5) Whom did Moses meet when he came to Egypt?
6) What did Pharaoh say to Moses and Aaron when he he was given God's message?
7) How did Pharaoh after that make the burden of the people heavier, and what did God say to Moses?

XXVIII
THE PLAGUES

Moses thereupon went to Pharaoh and warned him that unless he allowed the Hebrews to leave Egypt, one disaster after another would overtake the land. But the king took no notice of the warning, and ten plagues were brought upon the Egyptians, each more terrible than the other.

First, Aaron smote the water of the Nile and it changed into blood. The water could not be used for drinking, and all the fish died in it.

Next there appeared countless swarms of frogs in water and on land. This plague, too, was brought about by Aaron by striking the water of the Nile. These frogs were everywhere, in the houses, in the beds and even in the baking ovens. This time Pharaoh took notice, he was actually afraid. He summoned Moses and Aaron to him and said: "Pray to your God to remove these frogs that plague the people, and then I will let the Israelites go."

So Moses prayed to God that he take away the frogs, and God did so. But when Pharaoh saw that the frogs were no more, he changed his mind and would not let the people go. Then God punished Pharaoh a third time.

The third plague was a terrible one. Aaron smote the sand of the ground and ugly vermins came. They crawled all over, and they bit everybody. The people suffered very much, but Pharaoh would not give in.

The fourth plague consisted of flies. This plague as well as all that followed were brought through Moses. The king and his people suffered so much from the flies, that he again sent for Moses, and said to him: "Go and sacrifice to your God in the land" Moses said: "If we sacrificed animals to our God in Egypt the Egyptians will stone us; we must go to the wilderness."

Pharaoh said: "Remove this terrible pest from me, and I will let you go."

So Moses prayed to God, and the flies vanished from the land. But Pharaoh changed his mind again, when he saw that the flies were no more.

Then the fifth plague came. There broke out a disease among the cattle that belonged to the Egyptians. Many of the cattle died from this terrible disease. But Pharaoh remained stubborn and he would not let the people go.

The sixth plague was a fearful one. All the

Egyptians got great sores and boils all over their bodies.

Then the seventh plague came. This was a great hail storm. The hail fell in very big lumps. It destroyed the fruit on the trees and the grains in the field. It even killed some cattle, and even some people that were outside.

Pharaoh sent for Moses and Aaron and said: "I have sinned this time; the Lord is righteous and I and my people are wicked. Pray to the Lord and let him remove this plague from me, and I will let you go." Moses prayed to God and the hail ceased, but Pharaoh again withdrew his promise.

Moses and Aaron thereupon said to Pharaoh: "How long will you refuse to hearken to the God of the Hebrews. If you refuse to let the Israelites go, to-morrow God will send locusts upon your land; they will cover the whole face of the land, and they will eat up whatever grain was left from the hail." Moses and Aaron then left the king's palace.

The officers said to the king: "How long shall this man be a snare to us? Let the Israelites go to serve their God as they desire. Do you not see that Egypt is destroyed?"

Moses and Aaron were then brought back to

Pharaoh, who said to them: "Go and serve your God; but who are they that shall go?" Moses replied: "We will go with our young and with our old, with our flocks and with our herds we will go; for we must hold a feast to the Lord." "So be the Lord with you, as I will let you go," said Pharaoh. "Let only your men go and serve the Lord, for that is what you desire?" And Moses and Aaron were driven from Pharaoh's presence.

Then the eighth plague came which consisted of locusts. Insects, millions and millions of them, came into the land of Egypt. These insects, or locusts, ate up everything that was left after the hail storm.

Then the ninth plague came. This was darkness. For three days and three nights it was dark. It was so dark that the people could not see anything. They could not even see the candle light. There was no sun and no moon visible for three days.

After the ninth plague, Pharaoh called for Moses again and said to him: "I will allow you to go to the wilderness to worship your God, on condition that you leave your flocks behind in the land of Egypt."

Moses did not consent to this condition, and Pharaoh angrily said to Moses: "Get you from me, take heed to yourself, and see my face no more; for in the day you see my face you shall die."

Moses replied: "You have spoken well; I will see your face no more."

AGADAH

Unfaithfulness Punished

The Israelites were very happy to leave the land of their misery, although they knew that they would have to suffer a great deal before coming possessed of the promised land. But there were some Israelites who said: "Why should we leave Egypt where we have plenty to eat, and go through the wilderness and suffer want?"

God determined to put the grumblers out of the way, so that they discourage not the people, but the Egyptians upon seeing many Israelites perish, would say: "Lo, the Israelites, too, suffered death, it is evident then that it was not their God who has caused us all the trouble."

God therefore brought the plague of darkness, and under the cover of the darkness he slew all the wicked Israelites, and the Egyptians were not aware of what had happened.

QUESTIONS

1) Name the plagues thus far brought upon Egypt.
2) When did Paraoh say: "The Lord is righteous, and I my people are wicked."
3) Through whom were brought the first three plagues, and through whom were the rest of the plagues brought?
4) When did the officers urge Pharaoh to let the Israelites go?
5) What did Pharaoh then say to Moses, and what did Moses reply?
6) When was Moses driven out from the presence of Pharaoh, and why?

XXIX
FREEDOM

Thereupon God said to Moses: "One more plague will I bring upon Pharaoh and his people, and after this plague he will let you go out of his land. At midnight, I will cause the first-born of every family to die. Now tell the Israelites to be ready. Tell them to pack up their belongings, and be ready to go. Tell them to take a little blood from a lamb, and sprinkle it on the door-post of their dwellings. If they do that, no one in their houses will die. The angel of Death will pass over their houses."

Moses then sent messengers to all the people and told them to get ready to go out from Egypt.

At midnight, there was great terror in the land of Egypt. In every house, some one lay dead. Then did the cruel heart of Pharaoh relent. Pharaoh quickly called for Moses and said: "Come take your people and go! Go quick. Take everything with you and go! Don't wait. I don't want to see you any more in my land!"

Moses gave the order, and the people started to

147

move. They were in a great hurry to leave the land of their sorrow. They did not have enough time even to bake their bread. So the women took the dough, and when they were hungry they baked thin crackers (Matzoth) out of the unleavened dough. For this reason God told all the Jews to eat "matzoth," unleavened bread, each year during the holiday that is called Passover, Pesah.

At last the Israelites were free. They were slaves no longer. They were no more afraid of their cruel Egyptian officers. They marched out from Egypt with glad hearts. God told them that he would give them a good land which lay somewhere across the desert, a land flowing with milk and honey.

The Israelites marched towards the desert that lay between Canaan and Egypt. If they had kept along a straight course, they would have soon reached the land of their fathers, but Moses was afraid to follow too direct a route, lest they should be attacked by the Canaanites of the south. He therefore turned back and encamped near the Red Sea on the Egyptian border, at a point where stood the temple Baal-zephon, the Egyptian god of the desert.

The Egyptians, having forgotten the plagues, began to regret the loss of their slaves. When

Pharaoh's attention was called to the fact that the Israelites had turned back, he believed that Baal-zephon, the god of the desert, had caused them to go astray. He immediately set out with a big army and many horses and chariots in pursuit of the Hebrews to force them to return to Egypt and back to slavery.

Pharaoh overtook the Israelites encamping by the sea. The Israelites were greatly terrified at the sight of the enemy. Many of them even reproached Moses with these words: "Was it because there were no graves in Egypt, that you have taken us away to die in the wilderness? Why did you not leave us in Egypt?"

Moses consoled the people, saying: "Fear you not, stand still and see the salvation of the Lord. The Egyptians whom you see to-day, you shall see them again no more for ever."

And a miracle did happen for the Israelites. Just as the Israelites arrived at the shore of the Red Sea, a fierce easterly gale began to blow, beating back the water until the sea bed was visible, and the Israelites crossed to the opposite side of the narrow strait as though over dry land. The Egyptians tried to follow the Israelites, but at that time the wind ceased to blow, and the water surged back, swallowing the whole Egyptian army, horses, chariots, and all.

The Israelites from a distance saw the sea cover their old enemies and they sang a song of victory,

Miriam and Other Women Sang and Danced

praising God who had granted them freedom at last. Miriam, the sister of Moses, took a timbrel in her hands, and accompanied by other women, she sang and danced. And this was what they sang: "Sing to God, for he has triumphed! He has cast the horse and its rider into the sea."

The memory of the great deliverance from slavery is kept alive by the Jewish people even to this very day. From year to year they celebrate the Festival of Pesah, Passover, which begins with the fifteenth day of the month of Nisan and ends with the twenty-second day. They eat Mazoth, unleavened bread, during these seven days, to symbolize the hurried departure from Egypt.

AGADAH
The Trial

When God desired to drown the Egyptians, Uzza, the Angel of the Egyptians, drew near and said: "O Lord of the world! You are called just and upright; why then do you desire to drown my children in the sea?"

God then summoned all the angels, and said: "Judge you between me and yonder Uzza, the Angel of the Egyptians. In bygone days I brought famine upon his people, and my beloved Joseph, through his wisdom, saved them from destruction,

and they all became his slaves. But when my
children came into their land as strangers, they
were in turn made slaves by the Egyptians. My
children groaned under their heavy yoke, and I
sent Moses and Aaron, my faithful messengers, to
Pharaoh, to save them. When they spoke to him in
my name, he refused to listen to them. I punished
him, but he remained obstinate and he made the
yoke of the children of Israel still heavier and
their lives more bitter. Now when I redeemed
my children from his heavy yoke, he seeks to
destroy them."

When God had finished speaking, the heavenly
judges called out: "You, O Lord, are just in all
your ways, Pharaoh and his host deserve the
punishment you mete out to them."

Uzza heard their verdict, and he pleaded: "O
Lord of all the worlds! True, my people deserve
the punishment, but be you merciful and have pity
upon the works of your hand."

In an instant, Angel Michael flew to Egypt,
fetched a piece of a wall in which a Hebrew child
had been put in place of mortar, and standing with
it in the presence of God, said: "O Lord of the
world! Will you have pity upon this people who
killed innocent children so cruelly?" This silenced
Uzza, and God resolved to drown the Egyptians
in the sea.

The waters of the sea instantly began surging back, and the Egyptians were drowned. This happened at the hour of the morning when the holy hosts of heaven were wont to sing praises to the Almighty. They now gathered in great multitudes and were about to sing when God silenced them with the words: "The works of my hand are drowning in the sea, and ye desire to sing praises to Me?"

QUESTIONS

1) What was the tenth plague that God brought upon the Egyptians?
2) How were the children of Israel to be saved from the Angel of Death?
3) Why did God command the Israelites to eat *matzoth* on Passover?
4) Why did not Moses take a direct route on his way to the promised land?
5) What encouraged Pharaoh to pursue the Israelites?
6) What miracle occurred for the Israelites when they came to the Red Sea? And what happened to the Egyptians?
7) Tell what holiday we celebrate to commemorate the departure from the land of Egypt, and when and how it is celebrated.

XXX

FROM THE RED SEA TO SINAI

The Israelites were now free men, and led by their leader Moses, they marched towards the direction of the land of Canaan, the home of their ancestors, where they hoped to settle. When they reached the desert of Shur, they suffered greatly from thirst. At last they came to a place where there was some body of water, but the water was bitter and it was unfit to drink. They murmured against Moses, but their leader took some plants and cast them into the water, whereupon the water became sweet and drinkable.

In the course of their march they came to an oasis which had many springs and palm trees. This green spot was called Elim, beyond which lay the desert of Sin.

The provisions the Israelites had taken with them from Egypt were by this time exhausted and they began to feel the pang of hunger. They again reproached Moses and Aaron: "Would that we had died by the hand of the Lord in Egypt, when we sat by the flesh-pots, when we did eat bread to the full. You have brought us into the wilderness to kill the whole assembly with hunger."

Moses, in the name of God, announced to the people that in the morning they would be supplied with food sent down from heaven. And so it was. In the morning, the Israelites awoke to find the ground covered with some white substance, and Moses said to the people: "There is the food which God has given you to eat. You are to gather of it every morning, one measure for each person, and on the sixth day, you shall gather a double portion in order that you may have enough for the Sabbath day, when you are not permitted to gather it."

The Israelites gathered this white substance for their food, and they called it *manna*. Every morning it appeared afresh, and towards noon it melted in the heat of the sun. This food the Israelites ate throughout their wanderings in the desert for forty years.

When the Israelites reached a mountaneous country called Rephidim, they were attacked by a wild nomadic tribe, the Amalekites. Moses immediately got together his best men and put them under the leadership of his young disciple and lieutenant, Joshua ben-Nun. Moses accompanied by Aaron and Hur went up to the top of the hill from where he could be seen by the warriors.

When Moses held his hands up, Israel prevailed; but when he let them down, Amalek prevailed. As it was difficult for Moses to keep his hands up all the time, he sat on a stone, and his hands were supported by Aaron and Hur. Finally, Joshua, the young warrior repulsed the attack of the Amalekites and the Israelites continued their march.

After the lapse of about five weeks, the Israelites came to the desert of Sinai, and encamped near the mountain of Horeb (also known as Sinai, because it stands on the Sinai Peninsula). There Jethro, the father-in-law of Moses, hastened to meet Moses, bringing with him his daughter Zipporah, the wife of Moses, and her two sons. He was greatly pleased that the Israelites had at last gained their freedom.

While in the camp of the Israelites, Jethro noticed that Moses was kept busy day and night with the affairs of the people, settling their disputes. And Jethro said to Moses: "The thing that you do is not good. You will surely wear away, both you, and the people that is with you; for the thing is too heavy for you. Provide out of all the people able men, such as fear God, men of truth, and hating unjust gain. Place such men over the people to be rulers of thousands, of hundreds and tens, and let these men judge the people all the time, and appeal to you only in matters of great importance."

Moses followed the advice of his father-in-law, and chose from the people rulers to assist him in judging the people and settling their disputes.

———

AGADAH

The Manna Helps Decide a Case

Although manna would fall in tremendous heaps, yet no person could gather from it more than was required for the daily need of his family, and to each and every person was miraculously allotted an equal portion of it.

One day it happened that two Israelites came before Moses. One of them complained that the other had stolen his slave. The other denied the charge. Moses then said to them: "Come to me this evening and I will give you my decision." Then Moses visited the tents of the two men, counted the number of persons in each family and the number of manna rations that each family had gathered. When he found that the slave's ration of manna was found in the house of the complainant, he said to the other: "Return the slave to his rightful owner."

———

QUESTIONS

1) How was the water made sweet at Shur?
2) From where did the Israelites get their food in the wilderness?
3) Why did not the *Manna* fall on the Sabbath?
4) Who attacked the Israelites at Rephidim, and what was the outcome of the war?
5) Who was Jethro, and whom did he bring with him?
6) What was the advice that Jethro had given Moses?

XXXI
THE TEN COMMANDMENTS

In the third month after the Israelites left Egypt, the Israelites encamped near Sinai. Moses called the people together and said to them in the name of God: "You have seen what I did to the Egyptians, and how I bore you on eagle's wings, and brought you to myself. Now, therefore, if you will hearken unto my voice, and keep my covenant, then you shall be mine; and you shall be unto me a kingdom of priests, and a holy nation."

The people answered as one man: "All the Lord has spoken we will do."

Moses then told Israel to get ready for the third day to receive the Law of God. He ordered them to cleanse their bodies and their clothes so that they be fit to receive the holy Law. On the morning of the third day, Moses led all the Israelites out of their camp, and assembled them about the foot of Mount Sinai. He told them not to ascend the slopes of the mountain, and not to cross the boundery line which he had made around the mountain.

Then a dense smoke ascended from the mountain, and the mountain itself quaked. Thunder rolled and lightning illuminated the darkness. In the midst of this awe-inspiring sight, Moses alone ascended the mountain, and the people heard a mighty voice resound from the midst of the storm. They heard the very voice of God pronounce the ten divine Commandments of the Hebrew religion:

1.   I am the Lord your God who brought you out of the land of Egypt, out of the house of bondage.

2.   You shall have no other gods before me. You shall not make unto you a graven image, nor any likeness of any thing that is in heaven above, or that is in the earth beneath, or that is in the water under the earth; you shall not bow down to them, nor serve them.

3.   You shall not take the name of the Lord your God in vain.

4.   Remember the sabbath day, to keep it holy. Six days shall you do all your work; but the seventh day is a sabbath day to the Lord your God, in it you shall not do any manner of work, you, nor your son, nor your daughter, nor your man-servant, nor your maid-servant, nor your cattle, nor your stranger that is within your gates.

5. Honor your father and your mother, that your days may be long upon the land which the Lord your God gives you.

6. You shall not murder.

7. You shall not commit adultery.

8. You shall not steal.

9. You shall not bear false witness against your neighbor.

10. You shall not covet your neighbor's house; you shall not covet your neighbor's wife, nor his man-servant, nor his maid-servant, nor his ox, nor his ass, nor anything that is your neighbor's.

The people listened in awe to the utterance of the divine Commandments, and when the voice ceased they returned to their tents. But Moses remained on the mountain for forty days and forty nights. There God explained to him many laws which he was to teach to the children of Israel. Moses inscribed the Ten Commandments upon two stone tablets, and all the other laws he collected in a book which is known to this day as the Law of Moses, or the Five Books of Moses.

To commemorate the fact that God gave his people the ten commandments through Moses, the Jews to this very day celebrate the festival of Shabuôth, Feast of Weeks (*zeman mattan toratenu,* the time when our Law was given).

This festival is celebrated on the sixth day of

the third month, Sivan. It is called Feast of Weeks, because God commanded us to count seven weeks from the time the Omer (first ripe grain) was first brought into the Temple, on the second day of Passover, to the Shabuoth festival.

This holiday is the closing of the spring harvest which lasted in Palestine for seven weeks beginning with the second day of Passover. It began with the harvesting of barley on Passover and ended with the harvesting of wheat on Shabuoth. For this reason this festival is also known as the Festival of the First Ripe Fruit. On this festival, every land owner was to bring some of his first ripe fruit to Jerusalem, as a thanksgiving offering to God. To commemorate this harvest festival, we decorate our homes and synagogues with plants, flowers and trees.

AGADAH

The Heathens Refuse to Accept the Torah

Before God gave the Torah to Israel, he had offered it to every tribe and nation on the earth, so that hereafter they might not excuse themselves by saying: "Had the Holy One, blessed be he, preferred to give the Torah to us, we should have accepted it." He went to the children of Esau and said: "Will you accept the Torah?"

"What is written in the Torah?" they asked.

"You shall not murder is one of its commandments," replied God.

"Almighty God," they said, "do you desire to take from us the blessing which was given our father Esau? For he was blessed with the words: 'By your sword shall you live.' We do not want to accept the Torah."

Thereupon he went to the children of Ishmael and said to them: "Will you accept the Torah?"

"What is written therein?" the Ishmaelites asked.

"You shall not steal, is one of its commandments." said God.

"We cannot accept the Torah," they said, "because our father was blessed thus: 'His hand will be against every man.'"

God then went to all the other nations and all of them rejected the Torah because the commandments found in it were contrary to their own customs. He then went to the children of Israel and said to them: "Will you accept the Torah?"

"What is written therein?" they asked.

"The Torah contains six hundred and thirteen

commandments," said God. "Is it your wish to accept it or reject it?"

"All that the Lord has spoken we shall do and obey," they all said, as one man.

When God was about to utter the first word, nature stood still: the birds ceased their singing, wings became motionless, the billows of the sea were suddenly calmed, the streams stopped flowing, the angels stopped singing hymns, there was nothing but silence, both in heaven and on earth. The voice of God was then heard saying: "I am the Lord your God." Immediately the heavens and the earth were opened that they might serve as witnesses to the Israelites that there is none like God either in the heavens above or on the earth below. These words uttered by God himself were heard not only by the Israelites, but by all the nations of the earth.

QUESTIONS

1) What did God say to the people upon reaching Sinai?
2) What did the people reply?
3) Give the Ten Commandments.
4) What are the Five Books of Moses?
5) What holiday do we celebrate in commemoration of the giving of the Law?

XXXII
THE GOLDEN CALF

The people did not at once fully understand the doctrines proclaimed from Mount Sinai. There were many ignorant men who could not understand the existence of a Supreme Being or a God who could not be seen or touched. They could not at once be weaned from the worship of idols and other false beliefs they had learned in Egypt. When, therefore, Moses remained on the mountain they demanded of Aaron that he make them an image in the shape of a calf, like Apis, the sacred bull of the Egyptians.

Aaron at first refused to comply with their request, but finally he had to yield to their insistent demands and, out of the golden ornaments which they had brought to him, he melted down and cast into the form of a calf. Upon beholding the image, the people danced about it shouting: "This is our god who led us out of Egypt."

The people built an altar before their new god, and offered up cattle on it as sacrifices. They made merry, drinking and playing, after the fashion of idolators, while the sacrifices were offered.

God thereupon said to Moses: "Go, get you down; for your people, that you have brought out of the land of Egypt, have dealt corruptly. Now therefore let me alone, that I may consume them; and I will make of you a great nation."

Moses pleaded with God on behalf of the people and said: "Lord, why is your anger so kindled

The Golden Calf

against the people whom you have brought out from the land of Egypt? Why should the Egyptians say that you have brought them out of the land of Egypt to slay them in the mountains? Repent of the evil against your people. Remember Abraham, Isaac and Israel, your servants, to whom you did swear by your own self, and said to them: 'I will multiply your seed as the stars of heaven, and all this land that I have spoken of will I give to your seed, and they shall inherit it forever.'"

When God repented of the evil which he said he would do to his people, Moses descended the mountain, carrying with him the two stone tablets upon which God with his own hand had inscribed the Ten Commandments. At the foot of the mountain he met his faithful disciple Joshua waiting for him. Moses heard the sound of many voices coming from the camp of the Israelites, and together with Joshua, he hurried to camp. When he saw the people dancing around the golden idol, he flew into a great rage. He flung the tablets down and smashed them into fragments. Moses took the golden image, ground it to powder and threw the ashes upon the water.

Moses then cried out: "Whoever is for God, let him come with me." All the members of the tribe of Levi thereupon joined their great leader, for they had refrained from worshiping the golden calf. At the command of Moses, the Levites, armed with swords, attacked the idol worshipers, and slew many of them.

The anger of Moses against the people was short-lived, and he soon was praying again to God for mercy, saying: "Oh, this people have sinned a great sin, and have made them a god of gold. Yet, now, pray forgive their sin, and if not, blot me, I pray you, out of your book which you have written." And the Lord replied: "Whosoever has sinned against me, him will I blot out of my book."

God then taught Moses that he is merciful to every one who is sorry for the wrong he does. He also told Moses to prepare two stone tablets upon which he would again inscribe the Ten Commandments. Moses again stayed on the mountain for forty days and forty nights, at the end of which time he came down with other two tablets of stone upon which God himself inscribed the Ten Commandments.

AGADAH

The Strategy of Moses

Moses saw that God was determined to destroy Israel, and he made one last attempt to win mercy for his people. Turning to God he said: "Pray forgive this people for having made the idol; take the golden calf into heaven that it may assist you."

"What can the idol do, if I take it to heaven?" inquired God.

"You, O Lord, will send down the rain, and he will send down the dew. You will cause the wind and he will bring a cloud upon the earth," said Moses.

"Moses, are you mistaken like them," asked God, "and know not that the idol can do absolutely nothing?"

"If so," said Moses, "why are you angry with the people for having made that which is nothing?" Thereupon God withdrew his decree concerning the people of Israel.

———

QUESTIONS

1) Why did some of the Israelites demand an image in the shape of a calf?
2) What did the people exclaim when Aaron made a calf out of the golden ornaments the people had brought to him?
3) Where was Moses at that time, and what did God say to him?
4) Whom did Moses meet at the foot of the mountain?
5) What did Moses do with the tablets he brought down from Sinai?
6) How did Moses punish the people who worshiped the idol?
7) What did Moses do with the golden calf?
8) What took place after that?

———

XXXIII
THE TABERNACLE

When the people learnt something about God and his Law, God said to Moses: "Let them make me a sanctuary that I may dwell among them." Moses thereupon said to the people that he whose heart was willing should bring a gift for the building of the sanctuary. No one was forced to give, yet, so generously did their gifts pour in, that Moses was compelled to issue an order that they should send no more. The Jews freely gave of whatever they possessed towards the building of the Tabernacle. Princes gave gold and silver; others gave purple-dyed skins and other necessary material, while the women wove rich hangings and beautiful curtains. Everybody gave something towards the building of God's Tabernacle. In a short time the Tabernacle was completed under the supervision of the two very able architects, Bezalel and Oholiab.

When the Tabernacle was completed, at the extreme end of its interior there was a room separated from the rest by a curtain. In that room stood the arc decorated with two golden figures of cherubim (angels). The ark contained the two tablets upon which were inscribed the Ten Commandments. This room was known as the Holy of Holies. No one was permitted to enter this holy room save the high priest and that only once a year on the Day of Atonement. There was a seven branched golden candlestick in the sanctuary which was fed with olive oil and was kept continually burning. The whole Tabernacle was surrounded by a large court which was curtained. The building was so constructed that it could be taken apart and carried whenever Israel continued his journey.

In the first month of the second year after the departure of the Israelites from the land of Egypt, on the first day of the month, the Tabernacle was set up. Then a cloud covered the Tabernacle, and the glory of the Lord filled the holy structure.

By the decree of God, Aaron was appointed high priest of the Tabernacle and his sons were made priests. The high priesthood then became hereditary in the family of Aaron, passing from father to the oldest son. The rest of the tribe of Levi was set aside to do the service of God in the Tabernacle, assisting Aaron and his sons. They took apart the Tabernacle, carried it while Israel was on a journey, and set it up again when the camp came to rest. The learned and consecrated tribe of Levi thus became the teachers of the other tribes.

The Israelites celebrated the dedication of the Tabernacle for eight days, and on the eighth day, a fire came down from heaven and consumed the sacrifices which were prepared by the priests upon the altar. The people, upon beholding this great miracle, shouted for joy, and fell on their faces.

Now the two priests Nadab and Abihu, the sons of Aaron the high priest, took each his censer and put fire in it, and laid incense upon the fire. This was against the will of God, for he had ordered that no strange fire be brought into the holy place. So the two priests were punished: A fire came down from heaven and devoured them in the Tabernacle. Aaron began to complain of his loss, but Moses consoled him, and the bereft father held his peace.

Moses told Aaron and his remaining two sons that they must not lament or mourn their loss, and that they must not leave the sanctuary. He said that if they disobeyed this order it would spell death for them, because the anointing oil of the Lord was upon them.

———————

AGADAH

Moses Puts Together the Tabernacle

While the parts for the Tabernacle were under construction, some people who always like to find fault, complained that God had never commanded Moses to erect the Tabernacle. They claimed that Moses had done so of his own accord. But soon something occured that put a stop to such slanderous rumors.

When all the parts that went to make up the Tabernacle were ready, the wise man attempted to put the parts together, but were unsuccessful; several times did they put some parts together, but it fell apart again. Then Bezalel and Oholiab, the two master-builders of the Tabernacle, made an attempt to put the Tabernacle together, but in vain. Even they were unable to erect it.

The people were sorely disappointed and complained: "See what the son of Aaron has done to us. He assured us that God would descend from heaven and dwell among us in the Tabernacle. Now we have spent our money and went through a great deal of trouble, but it has all been in vain."

This report reached Moses and he too was disappointed, but he at once received the word of

God, saying: "Moses, you were grieved at the fact that you had no share in the erection of the Tabernacle. For this reason do I want all Israel to know that the Tabernacle cannot stand unless you set it up. Go therefore and set it up."

Moses had hardly put his hand upon the Tabernacle, when it rose of its own accord and stood erect. All the people marvelled at this great miracle, and the rumors among the dissatisfied elements in Israel concerning the erection of the Tabernacle, ceased forever.

QUESTIONS

1) What were the orders that Moses had issued with reference to the building of the Tabernacle?
2) Who were the two master architects of the Tabernacle?
3) Which room was known as the Holy of Holies, and what did it contain?
4) Who was appointed high-priest, and what were the duties of the tribe of Levi?
5) How were the offerings consumed on the eighth day of the dedication of the Tabernacle?
6) Give an account of the death of Nadab and Abihu, the two sons of Aaron.

XXXIV
IN ISRAEL'S CAMP

Moses introduced compulsory military service
in Israel, and every able bodied man over twenty
was compelled to bear arms, so that the Israelites
might be ready to repel possible attacks by the
wild nomadic tribes that wandered about in the
wilderness. Only the tribe of Levi, that was
wholly consecrated to the serive of the Tabernacle, was exempt from bearing arms and from
training for war. The number of those eligible
for military service was six hundred and three
thousand, and five hundred and fifty.

The entire camp of Israel consisted of twelve
tribes besides the tribe of Levi, the descendants
of Joseph having divided into two tribes, Ephraim and Manasseh. In the midst of the camp was
the Tabernacle, surrounded by the tents of priests
and Levites. All the other tribes surrounded the
tents of the Levites. The twelve tribes were ar-
ranged into four divisions, each consisting of three
tribes, having its own banner and its own indivi-
dual chief. Each of these four divisions occupied

a position to one of the four sides of the Levite square around the Tabernacle.

The Israelites Marching Through the Wilderness

The division of the tribe of Judah, which included the tribes of Issachar and Zebulun encamped east of the Tabernacle and journeyed first. On the south was the banner of the Reubenites, which included the tribes of Simeon and Gad. On the west was the division of Ephraim, which included the tribes of Manasseh and Benjamin. On the north was the division of Dan which included the tribes of Asher and Naphtali.

Whenever the Israelites were to break up camp and continue on their journey, the priests would blow their horns, and all the divisions would begin to move in the order in which they were encamped: the Levites, carrying the dismantled Tabernacle with the Ark, walking in the center, surrounded by the four divisions with their banners. During the day a cloud covered the Tabernacle, and in the night there was a fiery cloud. When the cloud moved, the Israelites followed it, and when the cloud tarried upon the Tabernacle the Israelites encamped. The Israelites stayed at camp as long as the cloud of glory remained over the Tabernacle.

There are several incidents of hardships and privations recorded in the Bible of Israel's journey through the wilderness. At one place the Israelites murmured against God, and they were punished for it. A fire from the Lord burned among them, and consumed some portions in the uttermost part of the camp. The people thereupon cried to Moses for help; and Moses prayed to God, and the fire abated. The name of that place was called Taberah (that is, *Burning*).

At another place, the mixed multitude of foreigners that was among the Israelites started to murmur against Moses, and the murmur was immediately taken up by all Israel, who wept bitterly and said: "O that we were given flesh to eat! We remember the fish, which we were wont to eat in Egypt for nought; the cucumbers, and the melons, and the leeks, and the onions, and the garlic; but now there is nothing at all; we have nought save the manna to look at."

The anger of the Lord was kindled greatly against the people; and Moses, too, was displeased. Whereupon Moses said to the Lord: "Why have you dealt ill with your servant? Why have I not found favor in your sight, that you lay the burden of all this people upon me? Have I conceived this people? Have I brought them forth, that you should say to me: 'Carry them in your bosom, as a nursing father carries the sucking child, to the land which you did swear to their fathers?' Whence should I have meat to give to all this people? I am not able to bear all this people myself alone, because it is too heavy for me. If you

choose to deal thus with me, I pray that you kill
me forthwith, and let me not look upon my wretch-
edness."

God said to Moses: "Choose seventy men of the
elders of the people, and bring them to the Tabernacle, and I will take of the spirit that is upon
you, and will put it upon them; and they shall bear
the burden of the people with you. And as for the
people, tell them that they shall have meat to eat,
that they shall have meat to eat for a whole month,
until it comes out of their nostrils, because they
have troubled me with their weeping, saying:
'Why, now, came we forth out of Egypt?'"

After having delivered God's message to the
people, Moses selected seventy men of the elders
of the people, and set them round about the Tabernacle. God thereupon descended in a cloud and
took some of the spirit that was upon Moses, and
put it on the seventy elders. The seventy elders
began to prophesy when the spirit rested upon
them, but they did so no more. But there remained
in camp two men, Eldad and Medad, who were
candidates for the office of Elders but had not
come to the Tabernacle, and these two men went
about in the camp prophesying.

A young man hurriedly came to Moses and informed him: "Eldad and Medad are prophesying in the camp." Joshua the son of Nun, the

minister of Moses, said: "My lord Moses, put them in prison." But Moses gently replied: "Are you jealous for my sake? Would that all the people of the Lord were prophets!"

On the same day a strong wind blew from the sea and brought across a very large number of quails in the camp. So eager were the people to taste meat, that they spent two days and one night in killing the quails and eating them. God was angry at the lustfulness of the people, and killed many of them with a plague. Yea, they died while the meat was yet between their teeth, before it was chewed. The name of the place where this incident occurred was called Kibroth-hattaavah (that is, *the graves of lust*).

At Hazeroth, Miriam and Aaron spoke against Moses because he had married a Cushite woman, and they said: "Has the Lord spoken only with Moses? Has he not spoken also with us?" Now Moses was the meekest of all men that ever lived upon the face of the earth. God suddenly spoke to Moses, to Aaron and to Miriam: "Let the three of you come to the Tabernacle." When the three arrived there, God spoke thus to Aaron and Miriam: "Hear now my words: if there be a prophet among you, I the Lord make myself known to him in a vision, I speak to him in a dream. This is not the case with my servant Mo-

ses; he is trusted in all my house; with him I speak
mouth to mouth, even openly, not in secret mes-
sages. Why then were you not afraid to speak
against Moses my servant?"

When the cloud was removed from over the
Tabernacle, Miriam was smitten with leprosy, she
became as white as snow. Aaron, upon beholding
his sister's terrible plight, pleaded with his brother
Moses: "O my lord, do not consider it as a sin
against us, for that we have done foolishly, and for
that we have sinned. Let her not be as one dead."
Moses thereupon prayed to the Lord: "Heal her,
now, O God, I beseech you."

God replied thus to the prayer of Moses: "If her
father had insulted her, should she not hide in
shame for seven days? Let her be shut up outside
of the camp for seven days, and after that she shall
be brought in again."

Miriam was accordingly shut up outside of the
camp for seven days. The people did not journey
till Miriam was brought in again, and thereafter
they journeyed from Hazeroth, and encamped at
Kadesh, in the wilderness of Paran, an oasis near
the border of southern Canaan.

QUESTIONS

1) Why was the tribe of Levi exempt from military service?
2) Describe the camp of Israel.
3) What happened when the people wanted meat?
4) Why did God tell Moses to appoint seventy elders?
5) Who were Eldad and Medad, and what happened to them?
6) What did Joshua advise Moses to do with Eldad and Medad and what did Moses reply?
7) What did God say to Aaron and Miriam when they spoke against Moses?
8) How was Miriam punished by God, and what did God say when Moses prayed for her?

———————

XXXV
THE SPIES

From Kadesh the Israelites sent twelve men, one from each tribe, to spy out the land of Canaan, and bring back word concerning its inhabitants, its soil and its vegetation. The tribe of Ephraim was represented by Joshua, the son of Nun, the faithful disciple and lieutenant of Moses, and the tribe of Judah was represented by Caleb, the son of Jephunneh.

The twelve spies traversed the land of Cannan from south to north and made themselves familiar with all the necessary details. When they arrived near Hebron, they took with them various fruits and also a large cluster of grapes which had to be carried on a pole by two men. The spies desired to show the fruit to their people on returning to camp.

After the expiration of forty days, the twelve spies returned to the camp of Israel at Kadesh and reported thus: "We came to the land whither you sent us, and surely ir flows with milk and honey; and this is the fruit of it. But the people that dwell in the land are fierce, and the cities are fortified and very great; moreover we saw the children of Anak (a giant tribe) there."

The Spies Took a Large Cluster of Grapes

The report of the spies was received by the Israelites in deep dismay. They wept bitterly, and some
of them even ventured to exclaim: "Let us appoint
a leader, and let us return to Egypt."

Joshua and Caleb, the only two spies who had
implicit faith in God, came forward and said that
their companions had failed to give a fair account
of the promised land. They tried to calm and console the dismayed people: "The land which we
passed through, is a very good land. If the Lord
is with us, you have no cause to fear its inhabitants. Only rebel not against the Lord."

But the people would not listen to the words of
the two brave men, and they wept bitterly the
whole of that night. Moses and Aaron fell on their
faces before the entire assembly of the children of
Israel, pleading for patience and trust in God, but
to no avail. Thereupon the glory of the Lord appeared in the Tabernacle and God said to Moses:
"How long will this people despise me? How long
will they not believe in me, for all the miracles
which I have wrought among them? I will smite
them with a pestilence, and destroy them, and will
make of you a nation, a greater and mightier people than they."

Moses replied: "When the nations will hear
of it, they will say: 'Because the Lord was not able
to bring this people into the land which he swore

to them, therefore he has slain them in the wilderness.' Now, I pray you, let the power of the Lord be great, as you have spoken, saying: 'The Lord is slow to anger, and abundant in kindness, forgiving iniquity and transgression.' Pardon, I pray you, the iniquity of this people according to the greatness of your loving-kindness, and according as you have forgiven this people, from Egypt even until now."

"I have pardoned according to your word," said God. "But say to them: 'As you have spoken in my ears, so will I do to you. You shall not come to the land, concerning which I lifted up my hand that I would make you dwell therein, save Caleb the son of Jephunneh, and Joshua the son of Nun. But the little ones, that you said would be a prey, them will I bring in, and they shall know the land which you have rejected. But as for you, your carcasses shall fall in this wilderness. Your children shall be wanderers in the wilderness forty years, until your carcasses be consumed, even according to the number of days it took you to spy out the land, a year for every day."

The people were displeased with the decree of God, and the more daring among them broke away from camp and rushed up to the mountains to attack the Canaanites and the Amalekites. But they were driven back by the inhabitants of the mountains suffering many losses. This failure brought the Israelites to submission, and they resigned themselves to their fate.

AGADAH
A Night of Tears

The spies employed every means of inciting the people into rebellion against Moses and God. On the following evening, every one of them went to his home, donned his mourning clothes, and began to weep and wail bitterly. When the household asked for the reason of such mourning, the answer was given: "Woe is me for you, my sons and my daughters, for you are doomed to fall by the hand of the Canaanites. The men that we saw there are strong and mighty and we dare not fight against them."

Thereupon the entire household burst into tears, and their neighbors came running to them, and upon ascertaining the cause of their weeping, they too joined in the wails, and thus it spread through the entire camp. When the sound of their wailing reached heaven, God said: "You faithless ones, you weep today without a cause, I shall see to it that in the future you shall have a cause to weep on this day."

So then it was that God decreed that the Temple be destroyed on the ninth day of the month of Ab, the very same day on which the Israelites wept in the wilderness without cause. This day became forever a day of tears.

———

QUESTIONS

1) How many spies did the Israelites send, and to what purpose?
2) What did the spies bring with them after forty days?
3) What was the report of the spies, and what was the effect upon the people?
4) Who are the two spies that tried to calm the people?
5) What did God say to Moses, and what was the reply given by Moses?
6) How did God punish the Israelites?
7) What did the people do upon hearing God's decree?

XXXVI
KORAH'S REBELLION

Soon another unpleasant incident occurred in the camp of Israel. Korah, of the tribe of Levi, and Dathan and Abiram of the tribe of Reuben, supported by two hundred and fifty important members of the various tribes, openly rebelled against Moses. They claimed that Moses and Aaron took too much power to themselves. "You take too much upon you," said the leaders of the rebels to Moses and Aaron. "All the congregation are holy, every one of them; wherefore then do you lift yourselves up above the assembly of the Lord?"

Moses sent to call Dathan and Abiram, but they refused to come, giving the insolent reply: "We will not come up; is it a small matter that you have brought us out of a land flowing with milk and honey, to kill us in the wilderness, but you must need make yourself also a prince over us?"

A great multitude gathered about the tents of the rebels, and the revolt seemed likely to spread. Moses, in the name of God, ordered the people away from the tents of the rebels. As soon as the multitude was at a safe distance from the tents, a miracle occurred; the earth, where Korah and his followers stood, opened up, and all the rebels, their tents and everything they possessed, were swallowed up.

But the people were still dissatisfied, and on the morrow they murmured against Moses and Aaron saying: "You have killed the people of the Lord." Instantly a plague broke out among the people, and many died in all parts of the camp. The heart of the ever-forgiving Moses, again yearned toward his people. He told Aaron to take his censer and offer an atonement for the people. Aaron stood with his censer between the living and the dead, and the plague was stayed.

God wished to further convince the people that he himself had selected Aaron to be high-priest. So he commanded that the head of each tribe take a rod, upon which the name of his tribe was to be written, and to place it in the Tabernacle. The name of Aaron was to be written upon the rod of the tribe of Levi. And it should be that the man whose rod blossomed was the one who was chosen by God. By this God desired to put an end to the murmurings of the children of Israel.

The rods were accordingly laid in the Tabernacle. To the amazement of all those assembled around the Tabernacle, the rod of Aaron was found on the following morning to bud, blossom and yield almonds. Everyone then acknowledged that Aaron was the chosen of God.

The Israelites continued to live in the desert around Kadesh for nearly forty years after the return of the spies. As a reminder of their life in the desert, the Israelites to this very day celebrate every year the Feast of Tabernacles (Sukkot). This holiday begins on the fifteenth day of the seventh month, Tishri, and continues for seven days. During these seven days we dwell in especially constructed tents. This holiday is also known as an agricultural festival, celebrating the harvest season, and is therefore called "Hag ha-Asiph."

For this reason we are told to take the four kinds of goodly trees upon which we pronounce benedictions, thanking God for the good harvest. The four kinds are: The Ethrog (citron), the Lulab (branches of palm trees), Hadasim (branches of myrtle trees), and the Araboth (branches of the willows of the brook).

The eighth day of this Festival is called Sh'mini Azeret, and the ninth day Simhat Torah—Rejoicing of the Law. On this day we conclude the reading of the Torah, and we also begin to read it all over again. Simhat Torah is a day of rejoicing and merrymaking. Everybody, even children, are called up on that day to pronounce the benedictions over the Torah. We also march around with the scrolls in the synagogue, to give people an opportunity to kiss the Torah. For the Torah is the only treasure that was left us from all our past glories.

QUESTIONS

1) What was Korah's complaint against Moses?
2) How were Korah and his followers punished?
3) What did the people say to Moses and Aaron on the following day?
4) How were they punished for that?
5) How was the plague stayed?
6) By what means was it proven again that Aaron was the chosen of God?
7) How many years did the people stay around Kadesh?
8) Why do we celebrate the festival of Sukkot?

XXXVII

WATERS OF MERIBAH. DEATH OF AARON

While the Israelites stayed at Kadesh, Miriam died, and she was buried there. The people once more suffered from lack of water, and they again murmured against their leaders: "Why have you brought the assembly of the Lord into this wilderness, to die there, we and our cattle? Why have you made us come out of Egypt, to bring us into this evil place, where there is neither food nor water?"

God thereupon said to Moses: "Take the rod, and then assemble the congregation, you, and Aaron your brother, and speak to the rock in the presence of the people, that it give forth its water, so that the people and their cattle have water to drink."

Moses and Aaron accordingly assembled the whole congregation of Israel before the rock, and Moses said to them: "Hear now, you rebels; are we to bring you forth water from this rock?" Moses thereupon raised his hand and smote the rock with his rod twice. Water gushed forth abundantly

193

from the rock and the people and their cattle drank.

God said to Moses and Aaron: "Because you believed not in me, to sanctify me in the eyes of the children of Israel, therefore you shall not bring this assembly into the land which I have given them." This is known as the waters of Meribah (that is, *Strife*).

From Kadesh Moses sent messengers to the king of Edom with a message: "Thus says your brother Israel: 'You know all the troubles that have befallen us; how our fathers went down into Egypt, and we dwelt in Egypt a long time; and the Egyptians dealt ill with us, and our fathers; and when we cried to the Lord, he heard our voice, and sent an angel, and brought us forth out of Egypt; and, now, we are in Kadesh, a city near your border. Pray, let us pass through your land; we will not pass through the field or vineyard, neither will we drink of the water of the wells; we will go along the king's highway, we will not turn aside to the right hand nor to the left, until we have passed your border.' "

Edom curtly replied to this polite plea: "You shall not pass through me, lest I come out with the sword against you." The children of Israel sent a message again: "We will go up by the highway;

and if we drink your water, we will pay for it; let us only pass on foot." To this message Edom replied again: "You shall not pass." And the king of Edom mustered his army and went out to meet the Israelites in battle. The Israelites, not wishing to engage in war with the Edomites, changed their course, and left the land of Edom behind them.

After that the Israelites journeyed from Kadesh, and when they reached mount Hor, God said to Moses: "Aaron shall now die, for he shall not enter the land which I have given to the children of Israel, because you rebelled abainst my word at the waters of Meribah. Take Aaron and Eleazer his son, and bring them up to mount Hor. Strip Aaron of his high-priestly garments, and put them upon Eleazar his son, for Aaron shall die there."

Moses, Aaron and Eleazar went up to mount Hor in the presence of all the children of Israel. Moses stripped Aaron of his garments, and put them upon Eleazar his son. Aaron died there on the top of the mount, and Moses and Eleazar descended from there. When the people saw that Aaron the high priest was no more they mourned and wept for him thirty days.

AGADAH

Aaron, the Beloved of the People

Ever since Aaron had realized that he had brought about the transgression of Israel by making the golden calf, he did everything in his power to atone for the sin. He would go from house to house and whenever he found one who did not know how to recite his prayers, he would teach him how to pray. If he found one who was unable to understand the laws of the Torah, he would explain them to him until he was able to understand them all.

The name "Peacemaker," which Aaron acquired among the Israelites, he well deserved, for he always strove to make peace among them. Whenever he found one who was extremely wicked and who would cause quarrels among relatives or friends, Aaron would visit him, become his friend, and teach him how to cultivate a kindly disposition. Never did he fail with his kind and peaceful disposition to influence his pupils.

If there was a quarrel between two learned men or between two ignorant men, Aaron was the one who would go about from one enemy's house to the other's until he succeeded in making peace between them. If there was a quarrel between a man and his wife, Aaron would visit their home daily, determine the cause of the quarrel, and then make peace between them.

When the people at the foot of the mountain saw Moses and Eleazer return without Aaron, they were greatly embittered. "It is impossible" they argued, "that a man who had once overcome the Angel of Death*) should now be overcome by him." They approached Moses and Eleazar and said to them: "Where is our beloved Aaron? What have you done to him? You had better return him to us, lest you die."

Moses prayed to God that he clear him and Eleazar of such baseless suspicion. God then said to the angels: "Lift up on high the bier upon which lies my beloved Aaron, so that Israel may know that he is dead and may not lay hands upon Moses and Eleazar."

The Angels opened the cave, brought forth the bier upon which Aaron lay and lifted it on high. All Israel then saw Aaron's bier floating in the air, and heard the angels proclaiming: "The law of truth was in his mouth; let him come in peace; let him come in peace."

---

* See page 138.

The Israelites, now convinced that Aaron was dead, wept bitterly for him and cried: "The pious has departed from our midst! Alas, the man of peace is no more!"

QUESTIONS

1) What happened upon the death of Miriam?
2) What did God tell Moses and Aaron to do?
3) How did they disobey God, and what was their punishment?
4) What did Moses request of the Edomites?
5) What was their reply?
6) Where did Aaron die, and who succeeded him to the high-priesthood?
7) Why was Aaron called *Peacemaker?*

XXXVIII
SIHON, OG AND BALAAM

The Israelites, were now near the border of the land of the Moabites, in the southeast of Canaan. Sihon, the mighty king, whose land extended along the eastern bank of the Jordan, had recently conquered a large portion of the land belonging to the Moabites.

Moses sent a polite message to Sihon asking for permission to go through his land but he too refused the request of the Israelites. Sihon marched out with a mighty army against Moses, and met with disastrous defeat at the hands of the Israelites. The victors thereupon entered the land and took possession of all important cities, including Heshbon, the capital.

The Israelites then proceeded farther north, into the land of Bashan, famous for its fine pasturelands. Og, the king of Bashan, a descendant of the ancient giants, came out with a mighty army against Moses. Encouraged by their first victory over the heroic Sihon, the Israelites fought bravely against the giant king, and defeated him badly. They took possession of this fertile land too, and thus the Israelites became the undisputed owners of Transjordania, the eastern part of Canaan.

Balak, the king of Moab, was very much afraid of the Israelites. He dared not get his army together and fight them in war, so he thought of a peculiar plan.

Not far from Moab there lived a man, whose name was Balaam. The people belived that Balaam possessed magic power to do wonderful things. So Balak, the king of Moab, sent for Balaam, and he asked him to come and curse the Israelites. Balak believed, that by cursing, Balaam could call upon evil powers to bring misfortune on Israel.

At first Balaam did not want to go. But when Balak sent for him again and promised to make him rich, Balaam saddled his ass, and started on his way to the king of Moab.

When the ass happened to pass a narrow path along a stone fence, it crouched and would not go any further. It pressed the foot of Balaam hard against the wall. Balaam suffered great pain, and he raised his stick and hit the poor ass three times.

The ass then said to Balaam: "Why are you cruel to me? You have ridden upon me many years, and I was always obedient to you. Why then do you strike me now?"

Suddenly Balaam saw an angel right in front of him, with a sword drawn in his hand. Balaam fell on his face in great terror.

The angel said: "I stood in the middle of the road. The ass saw me, and therefore would not go any further. Now when you go there to the king of Moab, be careful that you do not say anything bad about the people of Israel."

"O I have sinned," said Balaam. "If you want me, I will go right back again."

"No, you need not go back," said the angel. "You may go with these people who have come to call you. But be careful to say only what is good about the Israelites."

When Balaam came to the land of Moab, the king was very glad to see him. He took Balaam up to some high place from where he could see the whole camp of Israel. He then begged Balaam to curse the people.

Balaam was so much impressed with the orderly arrangement in the camp of the Israelites, that he blessed them instead of cursing them. Balak was very much disappointed, and he told Balaam to go right back to his own land.

———

AGADAH
Peace First

Sihon, the king of the Amorites, and his brother
Og, the king of Bashan, were the sons of Ahiah,
whose father Shemhazai was one of the fallen
angels. Sihon was a giant of marvelous strength,
and he was also very fleet of foot, and therefore
he was called Sihon, "foal," for his true name was
Arad.

Moses greatly feared to make war against this
giant and his mighty warriors. God assured Moses of victory, and Moses therefore no longer had
any cause to fear Sihon. But he nevertheless said:
"Let me send ambassadors of peace to Sihon to request him to permit Israel to pass through his
land."

"I commanded you to go forth and wage war
upon Sihon, and you wish to send ambassadors of
peace to him!" God reproved Moses.

"I have only followed your example, O Lord,"
replied Moses. "When it was your wish to deliver Israel from the land of Egypt, you could
have consumed the whole land with a flash of
lightning, yet you chose instead to send me to Pharaoh with a message requesting him to let the Is-

raelites go out of his land. And when it was your will to bestow your Torah upon the world, you offered it to the heathen nations before giving it to Israel."

"Your words have found grace in my eyes," said God. "Now therefore I command the children of Israel not to wage war hereafter upon any nation without first making it an offer of peace, and go to war only if the offer is refused."

QUESTIONS

1) Who was Sihon, and why did Moses wage war against him?
2) Against whom did Moses wage war after that?
3) For whom did the king of Moab send, and to what purpose?
4) What did the ass of Balaam do on the road, and why?
5) What did the angel say to Balaam?
6) Did Balaam curse the Israelites? If not, why not?
7) What did the king of Moab say to Balaam?

XXXIX
THE DEATH OF MOSES

The Israelites now made ready to cross the Jordan and conquer western Canaan. Representatives of the tribes of Reuben and Gad, the members of which were engaged in cattle breeding, and also half of the tribe of Manassoh, approached Moses, Eleazar the high priest, and the princes of the tribes, and said: "The land which our Lord God gave unto us as a possession on this side of the Jordan is good pasture land, and your servants are possessors of many cattle. It is our request that this land be given to the tribes of Reuben, Gad and half the tribe of Manassoh, and that you do not take us across the Jordan."

Moses reproachfully replied: "Shall your brethren go to war, and shall you stay here? If you will agree to send your able-bodied men, who are capable of bearing arms, across the Jordan to help your brethren conquer western Canaan, then you will be granted possession of this land."

The representatives of the two tribes replied: "All we wish to do is to build sheepfolds here for our cattle, and towns for our little ones, but we ourselves are ready to take up arms and fight in the ranks of the Israelites across the Jordan. We will not return to our homes until all the people have been settled and are in peaceful possession of the land across the Jordan."

So Transjordania was allotted to the tribes of Reuben, Gad and half the tribe of Manasseh, and the rest of the tribes had to cross the Jordan before they could gain possession of western Canaan. But at this time, the great leader and liberator of Israel felt that his end was approaching. He knew that he was not destined to complete the task he had begun, and that he would never lead the people into the promised land.

In his last days, Moses called the Israelites together and taught them the Law of God. He exorted them to live in their new land according to the principles of justice and freedom and brotherly love. He then appointed Joshua to be the leader of the Israelites in his stead.

Before his death, Moses blessed each tribe separately, and told the people what would happen to them in the future. After that he ascended to the top to Mount Nebo, a peak of the Pisgah range, from where he could see almost the whole country that lay across the Jordan. On the top of this mountain the great leader stood for some time, profoundly impressed by the view which spread before him. His heart was full of grief and sorrow that he should not have been allowed by God to enter the future domain of Israel.

Moses Ascended to the Top of Mount Nebo